Stay in the Game

Jared Veldheer's Journey to the NFL

—

Written by Andy Losik in association with Jim and Mary Veldheer

Front cover photo by Bruce Yeung, Chandler, AZ

Back cover photo by Kelsey Riggs, WCNC TV, Charlotte, NC

Proceeds from this project benefit programs that support aspiring athletes, helping them *Stay in the Game.*

Author's Note

In your hands you hold a project that has spanned five years. These 27,000-plus words have been a truly team effort. It took us awhile but we think we finally got it right.

Outside of being a massive human being, there is nothing cliché about Jared Veldheer's path to the National Football League, and that's why this book took a while to fully develop. My passion for the game and deep admiration for the work ethic and tenacity that Jared has for life have kept me focused on getting this book into the hands of future readers.

Special thanks to Jim and Mary Veldheer who desire to share some of the key elements that have made their son so successful in hopes this work may entertain and inspire young and not-so-young readers. This book can also serve as a bit of a roadmap for parents of potential professionals as they navigate "the process" of becoming an actual

NFL player.

Thanks especially to all of my wordsmithing friends for their feedback and proofreading skills. Thanks to Brad Monastiere at Hillsdale College for his help in historically verifying facts from Jared's time at the Division II school. Thanks to all of the high school, college, and professional coaches and athletes who helped with telling this story. Their admiration for Jared was evident in their eagerness to assist. Thanks to my parents for their never-ending enthusiasm.

For Kim and Kasey, whose enduring encouragement was invaluable in helping me "stay in the game" and complete a story that needed to be told. ~ AL

Forward

"Aren't you so proud of your son?" "You must be so proud!" "How exciting!" "You must be great parents!" "Don't you just love game day?" "Did you ever think that your child would be in the NFL?"

We've heard them all. All the comments and questions regarding having a son who has grown to be an NFL left tackle. Yes, we are proud of Jared, but maybe not in the manner some would think. Jared is my first-born child. I have also been blessed with a kind and smart step-son Aaron who came to our marriage with my husband Jim. The frosting on the cake was being blessed with a beautiful and loving daughter named Meghan!

Each of those questions posed earlier apply to each one of them. They all participated in sports through college, and game day was always exciting. While pride in a "cocky" sense has never been our thing, we are proud of not only their talents but the way they conducted themselves as teammates. We can honestly say that one child's achievements don't put them any higher on our love list. As for being great parents, that's funny. God blessed **us** with great kids. They are kind and loving people. Our job has been to love and care for children He entrusted to us.

"Stay in the Game" is a story of a big baby growing into a big boy who later grows into a big man. But there are many big people in the world, and they don't all play NFL football. As a young boy, we never would have dreamt that to be Jared's future. He was a kind child. Not rough or aggressive. He was not a follower. He liked thinking for himself. That really wasn't always a good thing for a parent trying to get their son to follow their directions. But, we knew in the long run, thinking for himself would be a positive quality.

Being the center of attention was never Jared's goal. He was NOT a social butterfly. Jared might not have liked sports at all if his dad and older brother hadn't been so sport minded. This is a story of a boy who liked candy, junk food, puzzles, video games and Legos. He kept his room a mess. This is a story of a boy who has a loving heart that is much larger than his body. This is a story about a boy who was always bigger than his peers often leaving him feeling like he didn't quite "fit in." Being bigger, meant being a bit slower. This is a story about a pre-teen boy who was athletically slower than his peers. This is a story about a child, who early on, usually made the "B" team. Regardless of his "B" team status, he would play with the heart of a lion (even if the lion was physically a little slower than the other lions!)

"Did it hurt to watch your son struggle?" Now that would be a great question! YES IT DID. Most parents hurt when they watch their kids struggle. But struggle isn't always bad. So to all the moms and dads reading this story, if your child struggles, regardless of what is causing the struggle, stay focused on the love you have for YOUR child. Support their effort. Don't give in to the temptation to compare your child to other children. Children will do that themselves...so will their teachers, coaches and other parents. Make home a sweet place to fall. And remind them over and over, that God Has A Plan For Them. It's not preachy, it's true.

To all the kids reading this story, quit comparing yourself to other kids! Enjoy your childhood. Love your family. Work hard in school. Explore your talents and then work to develop that talent. Stay active and enjoy playing on a team. Be a loyal friend. And when that day comes when you doubt yourself, remember that God Has A Plan For You Too! He really does.

Jared, it has been one life's greatest blessing being your mom and dad.

~Jim and Mary Veldheer

Chapter 1: Five Key Principles

There were thirty seconds left in the game and Oakland fans were in a frenzy. Trailing by three points, a long pass had just put the Raiders into field goal range, and it looked like this game was headed to overtime.

After the initial roar, a murmur set over the Coliseum as all eyes turned toward the yellow flag lying in the backfield. It sat dead-on in the telltale spot for offensive holding.

"Holding...Number 68...offense," the referee announced.

Jared Veldheer, Oakland's rookie tackle had grabbed too much of a Kansas City Chief and had gotten caught. As the referee marched off the ten yards from the spot of the foul and a chorus of "boos" rained down on a chilly Bay Area winter afternoon, Veldheer faced two choices. He could listen to the boos and have them zap his concentration or choose to "flush it."

"Forget the last play, whether it is good or bad. Forget it," coaches had preached over and over.

If a player is celebrating a big catch or dwelling on a mistake, he isn't thinking about the coming play and is likely to mess it up.

"Flush it," Jared told himself.

On the next play, Jared stepped up to the line and faced Tamba Hali, one of the best defensive players in the game. This time he kept the Chief's defensive end in front of him, allowing his quarterback enough time for another deep pass back into field goal range.

Not only would the Raiders push the game to overtime, they would eventually win 23-20.

If Jared had let that penalty distract him, a wily veteran like Tamba Hali would have eaten him for lunch and taken advantage of a younger player. The Chiefs would have been able to crush the final drive and never allow the Raiders to get to overtime, let alone win the game.

It is that kind of mental toughness and belief in making the right decisions that has helped Jared Veldheer get where he is today. Being able to set aside a failure and move forward is not just a trait of a successful football player; it can help anyone become successful doing anything they want to tackle.

That play was just one of the countless positive decisions that Jared Veldheer has made in both his football life and his personal life, far too many to list in a book. Most though can be narrowed down to five key principles.

1. God has a plan for your life.
2. Choose your friends wisely.
3. Listen to your coaches and those you trust. Tune out all the other noise.
4. Set goals. Track your goals. Achieve your goals.
5. Learn from your mistakes but don't dwell.

Chapter 2: One Big Boy

Although Jared Veldheer is one of the quickest linemen in the NFL, nothing on his road to pro football came quickly, not even his birth. After twenty-seven hours of labor, Mary Veldheer gave birth to twelve pound Edwin Jared Veldheer on June 14, 1987. Not only was he big, but he also had an appetite to match.

Mary's doctor suggested she offer her newborn son four ounces of formula at a time. Mary filled up an 8-ounce bottle planning to save the leftovers after they saw how much Jared would take. The whole eight ounces was gone before anyone knew what had happened!

Jared's mom calls it "mad hunger" and points out that the future football star found having to be burped after every couple of ounces a big inconvenience. Jared was one easy baby to please —just keep his belly full.

At around nine months, the big toddler built his first

blocking sled. The Veldheers had heavy oak chairs in their kitchen, and when he thought no one was looking, Jared would sneak away and spend as much time as he could pushing those big chairs. He would have to crawl to the kitchen, but once he pulled himself up, glimpses of the run blocking strength that made him a starter as a rookie were evident. All of that leg driving and the hours he would spend bouncing in his crib had him walking by ten months.

Jared also showed he had a sensitive side early on. He liked to be rocked, and once he could talk a little, Jared would croak out the words "back rub" when Jim or Mary would put him down to sleep. It is fair to say he was a gentle giant even then, and if you spend much time with him now, you get the same impression.

Along with that gentleness came a quiet toughness. You have to have a pretty high tolerance for pain to handle the collisions an NFL lineman must endure. Growing up, Jared never was one to complain much about pain. In fact one time Mary took him for his yearly "well baby" visit and the doctor discovered the future Raider and Cardinal had dual ear infections. She and Jim had no idea he wasn't feeling well based on his appetite, mood, or behavior. That is the kind of guy you want on your football team: one that doesn't gripe too much about being sore and presses on just the same.

Little Jared soon began to show evidence of a mental toughness. The "terrible twos" were actually pretty tame around the Veldheer household, but when Jared hit three an all-pro stubborn streak was born.

As tough as some of Jared's match-ups have been on the football field, none could match the mental battles he and his mother would engage in during the summer of 1990. Tamba Hali might be a lot bigger, faster, and stronger but he has nothing on Mary when it comes to matching wits with a three-year-old. When Jared knew he wanted something, there was no changing his mind. There was no changing Mary's mind either, even if her young son was acting like a lunatic in the grocery store. The Veldheers were fair but consistent and every punishment fit the crime.

Chapter 3: Nobody's Fool

This is the point where many professional athlete biographies switch to typical stories of how the only toy the kid ever wanted to play with was a football or how he tackled everyone and everything including grandma and the family dog.

That is not part of the life story of Jared Veldheer, because Jared was much more of a thinker than a tackler. He never broke the neighbor's window with a ball from fifty yards away. Nope, he was too busy either building with Legos or chasing some critter through the backyard. Jared was a builder and loved all kinds of puzzles. He could get seemingly lost for hours in one project. He would follow the directions that came with the Legos instead of just aimlessly mashing them together. Everything had an order and a purpose and that carried over to how he made friends.

Jared liked time alone with his own stuff, but that doesn't mean he was scared of playing with other kids. He just needed to have a reason for it. The kids that Jared wanted to hang out with were the ones that could think right along with him on whatever great invention or plan he was hatching. One summer in elementary school, the Veldheers signed Jared up for day camp. Jim and Mary wanted him to play with more kids but were worried he might be scared or nervous. As Mary was driving him up to the welcome area and the gaggle of kids gathered, she offered one last out to Jared.

"You don't have to do this if you don't want," she said.

"No mom, it's okay," the future All-American said as he hopped out of the car.

Jared had a good time at the camp and every night he was full of stories of the day's happenings. Jared really enjoyed doing his favorite kinds of things with other kids who were into them as well.

The Veldheers realized early on that they didn't have

much to worry about with Jared when it came to him ending up in some pickle just because other kids wanted to do something dumb. That stubborn streak that was so tough on his mom and dad at age three was now a positive. Jared Veldheer was nobody's fool and nobody was going to make him do something he knew was not right.

Chapter 4: The Right Kind of Friends

Some of Jared's closest friends, even to this day, are ones he made shortly after his family moved across town from the west side of Grand Rapids, Michigan to Ada.

Jared started his new school in fourth grade and quickly hit it off with a pair of rough-and-tumble twins—Mark and Derek Ehnis. Jared liked Mark and Derek, and together they would go on bicycle adventures up the street for candy. They made Jared's move to the new neighborhood easy, and Jim and Mary knew right away these were the type of kids they wanted as friends for Jared.

The Ehnis twins were a couple of sports nuts whose sibling rivalry had made them ultra competitive and they were a big reason why Jared began playing organized sports. Jared's brother Aaron was the other reason. Aaron was always hitting, throwing, catching, shooting, or dribbling some type of ball.

Aaron is nine years older so the two didn't play much together, but just having a brother like that in your home keeps athletics on the front burner.

Jared went to a few basketball camps when he was young and that ignited a passion for the game. When he was in the fourth grade it was time to start playing for real. Dad, Jim, was the coach and the Ehnis twins were Jared's teammates. Jared loved playing basketball, but it wasn't easy for him. He was always head and shoulders taller than the rest of kids in the program, but coordination gave him trouble when it came to keeping up with the smaller, quicker players. Jared played hard but was never a star on any of those teams. In fact, in 7th and 8th grade basketball at school, Jared was selected for the "B" team.

This may have bothered his parents but Jared paid no attention, focusing his efforts on playing the game, working hard, and listening to his coaches as they tried to teach him the game.

There were other sports in Jared's life. Football began in the Forest Hills Youth Football League at age ten. Jared was in the 5th grade, and his coach was Bob Stead who had played at the University of Michigan. Bob was a great head coach, but it wasn't Coach Stead that left the lasting impression. Jared's lasting memory of that team came via an assistant coach who loved to make the players run. During practice he had them run laps, run sprints, run up and down hills, run, run, run. Jared liked football but really hated running. He still does!

Fortunately for Jared, football did get better as a sixth grader. The coach was his buddy Jake Gratser's dad. In one game late in the season, Coach Gratser gave Jared the chance to carry the football. It was late in the fourth quarter and his team was winning by three touchdowns. Jared was understandably pumped! Never before had he been given an opportunity to run with the ball. His excitement had never been higher as he anxiously waited for his number. The fun came to a screeching halt when Jared bumped into the quarterback and fumbled away the handoff. At the age of eleven, Jared had a tough time shaking off that disappointment.

Jared might have had a rough go at running back, but that same year he began to show the first signs of dominance in another sport. Maybe having his own foosball table in his basement at home was part of the reason, but no one at Northern Trails Elementary School could keep up with him during noontime foosball tournaments. Jared's first championship in any competition was the 1998 Northern Trails Foosball Doubles title. His teammate was Mark Ehnis.

Chapter 5: Nothing Is Easy

People can argue whether foosball is really a sport or not. But what they can't argue is the fact that whatever new activity or competition Jared tried, he usually ended up being pretty good at it. Yet that doesn't mean it always came easy.

Just before Jared started the seventh grade, the family went to visit their friends who lived on a lake near Detroit. Adam Cheslin, the dad, asked Jared if he would like to learn to water ski. Adam patiently drove the boat and hollered out instructions on how to get up. After about fifteen or twenty attempts, the Veldheers were back on the dock thinking water skiing might not be in Jared's future. Jared was disappointed that he couldn't get his big body out of the water and up on skis, but he didn't give up on the idea completely.

A few years later when the Veldheer family bought a boat, Jared gave wake boarding a shot. This adventure went much better. Today, at over 320 pounds, Jared can pull off maneuvers behind a boat that most people can't believe.

Another adventure Jared wanted to tackle was snowboarding. Jim says it nearly broke his heart to see Jared getting dragged up the hill by the towrope time after time after time. A few friends from school were there too and they gave Jared a few snowboarding tips. Even though those tips didn't pay off that night, on his next trip to the slopes Jared looked like he had been snowboarding for years.

Jared's "stay in the game" perseverance during his middle school years would pay off his entire life. A lot of kids would have given up on water skiing or snowboarding after the first few failures. Jared just learned from them.

The scientific mind of Jared Veldheer is a lot like the scientific mind of Thomas Edison who said, "I haven't failed. I have just found 10,000 ways that will not work."

This trait would develop slowly but steadily throughout Jared's younger years.

Life at times was also emotionally painful for Jared. It can get pretty rough when you are bigger and heavier than all of the other kids.

The middle school years are tough for everybody, even the kids who seem the coolest. Jared's large frame made him feel awkward and different at times. All anyone wants at that age is to be accepted and to "fit in." Jared's size made feeling that way difficult. Even when your closest friends include you in all of their plans, there are those moments you can't escape feeling embarrassed. There are the times when you sit down in a chair and break it. There are times when none of the uniforms are big enough for you.

There are times when you just want to sit in the back row, to become invisible. Grown-ups tell their kids that it is no big deal and to not let anything bother them. That is a whole lot easier said than done.

One summer Jared was so self-conscious about his body not being naturally trim and muscular like the other boys, that he wouldn't even take off his shirt at the pool or at the lake. Finally after countless attempts at trying to convince Jared to be himself and not to worry about it, Mary scheduled a visit to the pediatrician.

Sometimes kids just need to hear a message from someone other than their parents and she figured a doctor would carry a lot of clout in Jared's world.

The doctor explained that in males there is a chemical called testosterone and that the body starts producing large doses to transform your body from a boy to a man. The doctor told Jared that his just hadn't kicked in yet and that when it did Jared wouldn't believe the results.

Mary told Jared to just hang in there and to

remember what the doctor had said.

She then lovingly added, "Jared, God has a plan for that big body, and I can't wait to see what it is."

No one could have guessed just how big that body would get nor that someday it would help take him to the NFL. In the meantime, Jared would just have to accept being bigger than everybody else and maybe even find ways to start using it to his advantage.

If there is a sport where it would be easy to be self-conscious, it is swimming. Mary was a gifted swimmer in high school. When Jared was a teenager, the local swim team needed older kids for competitions to add points to the team's total. Jared's younger sister, Meghan, was already a competitor on the swim team, so Mary encouraged him to join the team. He gave it a try and at times Jared finally found his big frame came in handy.

Although he kept his Speedo trunks hidden until the last possible second before climbing upon the starting blocks, Jared's hit created rough seas for the competition. Mary said he didn't have the best technique but he made up for it in effort. His effort sent ripples so big off to the sides that if he was a boater he would be picking up a ticket in a "no wake" zone. Jared didn't win many races, but he did pick up some ribbons and help the club's relay team. Mary was extra proud because she knew swimming was a sport that put all of those things Jared had been trying to hide on display. He kept at it anyway.

In their most successful endeavor, Mary and Jared struck gold in the Egypt Valley Country Club Mother-Son golf tournament when Jared was thirteen. In the tournament moms and sons had to take turns hitting shots and there wasn't a kid in West Michigan who could hammer a drive like Jared Veldheer. The pair made quick work of the competition as they burnt up and down the golf course. Being bigger and stronger was a big advantage for Jared, and he didn't have to wear a Speedo to do it either.

The first trophy Jared Veldheer ever won came on that afternoon. Mary thinks Jared won something even bigger that day, an acceptance that his size is just who he is. Life even seemed to get a lot more enjoyable after that. Some people spend their entire lives trying to understand that fact. Jared was starting to really "get" it just as he was entering high school.

As you have read, Jared could have given up easily on a lot of things. But there were few, if any, times that he did. "Staying in the game" would bring him many dividends on the football field and beyond.

Chapter 6: A Player Develops

When Jared entered Forest Hills Northern High School as a freshman, varsity football Coach Brent Myers described him as "pretty tall but scrawny." By his senior year and after a bundle of growth spurts, Jared had filled out into an offensive lineman who was attracting attention from some of the biggest programs in college football.

There wasn't anything really special that Jared did during those high school years. He followed Coach Meyers' football weight lifting program and he did some speed and agility work with John Baker at Extreme Performance. Through natural development and maturity, that tall and scrawny kid grew to 6 feet 7 inches tall and nearly 280 pounds. A lot happens between entering high school as a fourteen-year-old boy and leaving as an eighteen-year-old adult. There is absolutely no way to tell how each individual will mature along the way.

If you had watched the freshman Forest Hills Northern Husky football team in 2001 you probably would not have been able to pick out who the future third round NFL draft pick would be. Most would guess one of the starters. As a freshman, Jared didn't start a single game. Sure, he got to play in spots, but it wasn't until about halfway through his sophomore year that he would get his first start with the junior varsity team.

This may have been the end of the book if Mary hadn't intervened. You see, just before his junior year in high school Jared told his parents he didn't want to play football anymore. Mary dug a little deeper as to why, and Jared said he wasn't looking forward to football camp where they feed you bad food, make you sleep in a small bed, and run practice all day long. To which the quick-thinking Mary said, "Well, if you are not going to play football then you have to play soccer or run cross country. You like to eat all the time and you will have to find a way to keep that body fit and healthy." It didn't take long for Jared to figure out football was the best option.

When Jared joined the varsity team under the lights on Friday night, he bounced between tight end and tackle. It wasn't until the middle of his junior year that he became a starter. Think about it, a future pro athlete was neither a star nor a starter for most of his high school football career. This is why "staying in the game," no matter what game, is very important. You don't know how good you will become until you give it your best shot. Your best shot includes learning the game, giving your best physical effort, and giving yourself the proper amount of time to achieve success.

As a junior in high school Jared stood 6 feet 6 inches tall and weighed 255 pounds. As the coming years would prove, he was just getting started size wise.

The team only won three games that year, but as far as his development as a football player was concerned, he had achieved monumental gains since those days on the freshmen team. College coaches started to take notice of Jared and stopped by FHN to begin recruiting conversations with him and his coach. Regional recruiting coordinators from Purdue University, Michigan State, and Notre Dame all extended invitations for on-campus visits.

With football done for another year, Jared was able to focus on the sport he truly loved—basketball.

Unfortunately, Jared would miss part of the season when he broke a bone in his foot. The 2003-2004 Husky basketball team went 14-7.

Chapter 7: Really Big Man on Campus

Soon it was the end of summer and football season again. Before the year even kicked off, Jared's size and glimpses of excellent play from were beginning to put him on more colleges' recruiting radars. He was featured in the 2004 Grand Rapids Press football preview insert with news of Michigan State, Notre Dame, and Stanford all showing interest. None of that really mattered to Jared. He and his teammates tried to focus on the upcoming season.

At the start of the 2004-2005 school year, a big change came to Forest Hills, one that would have a big effect on Jared and his teammates' football season and ultimate success. That year the school district opened their third high school, Forest Hills Eastern. The majority of students that were redistricted came from Forest Hills Northern, which included many Northern football players.

The team didn't lose too many players that had been

counted upon as upcoming starters, but it did lose valuable backup and practice players. Instead of having sixty players on the varsity team, the Huskies started the year with thirty players. At one point, the team would dress twenty-four due to injuries. As a result, many players would be on both offense and defense, an exhausting situation.

On the offensive side of the ball, Jared began his senior season starting at left tackle, later moving to tight end. In addition to playing on the defensive line, he would also move to center after the starting center broke his leg. At over 6' 7" now, Jared was the tallest center in the state of Michigan, and over the course of the season would prove to be one of the best run-blockers in the area.

After the season ended, Jared was named a First Team All-Conference offensive lineman by the coaches. He was also named to the defensive line Second Team All-Area by the Grand Rapids Press. Accolades never seemed to mean much to Jared, so he wasn't too disappointed when the All-State teams were announced and he hadn't even garnered an honorable mention. Creston's Cam Bradfield didn't even make the All-Area team. By "staying in the game," neither man would trade their path to the NFL for awards not received in high school.

It was now time for Jared to move on to basketball and what would be a memorable season at Forest Hills Northern. After showing great potential and promise as juniors, nine seniors, each with their own unique talents, returned with high expectations for the 2004-2005 season.

One of the greatest tributes to Jared's keys for success was played out during his senior basketball season.

At 6' 7" and 255 pounds, Jared looked like a giant on the court. That bulk created a challenge for him and held him back in the up-tempo game FHN played. His teammates included a 6' 6" Bosnian named Pedja Lazic, who had great basketball skills. The rest of his teammates were fast and athletic (including All-State forward Travis Worst). Given the amount of talent around him, Jared was often relegated to the bench. The team ended up with an impressive record of 19-4.

Three big games were played that year against the highly rated and backyard rival, Forest Hills Central Rangers. FHC won the first game with Jared logging most of his minutes on the bench. The second game, at FHC, had a much better outcome. The Rangers would carry a two-point lead into the second half with the Huskies winning 55-51 to advance their record to 16-3. A huge key that sparked FHN was the combined "twin tower" play of Jared and Pedja. On the night, the two would combine for thirteen points and thirteen rebounds underneath and in the paint. Jared would get ten of those points himself, marking his first jaunt into double figures for the season. This team win handed Central its only league loss of the year. Both teams figured they'd meet again come tournament time and it looked like Jared and the Huskies had found a key to victory in utilizing their two big men.

As expected, ten days later the two teams would meet for a third time in the district championship game of the state tournament.

Most would figure that Northern would employ the

"twin tower" strategy that forged the big win on Central's floor ten days earlier, especially with any loss now meaning elimination. However, in the games since their big win over Central, the Huskies had played a smaller line-up using more guards and playing mainly with Pedja underneath. Jared had a combined four points in the last two games and really hadn't seen the floor much at all. This new strategy was doing the job until the night of the district finals.

Northern continued to play "small" and Forest Hills Central won easily on its way to the district title, advancing to the regional level of the state tournament.

Many questioned why the coaching staff had abandoned what had worked so brilliantly the last time the two schools met. Jared never questioned his coach. Jim Veldheer now says that it was really Jared who taught him and other parents something profound about life that night.

"In that loss, we as parents learned a huge lesson from our son. Listen to your coaches. Don't question the coach's plan, for it is his game plan that a team must follow. The person who never expressed a bit of doubt in the coaching staff or anger over playing time was Jared. He did what he was asked, letting the coaching staff determine how he was to be used."

For Jared the real disappointment came with the fact that he was finished playing organized sports with his hometown friends. These guys, Jared's teammates, were what really kept him engaged in playing sports — well, other than his fear of having to run cross country.

Many of Jared's football and basketball teammates are still friends today. Travis Worst earned a college basketball scholarship at Hillsdale College and was Jared's freshman roommate. Pedja Lazic went on to become a two time All-American at NAIA Aquinas College and now plays basketball professionally overseas.

It was time to move on to college athletics for Jared. He had "stayed in the game" and had chosen the right kinds of friends who had supported him through the ever-changing middle school and high school years. He had listened to his coaches and was finally realizing that God indeed did have a plan for that big body. That body wasn't done growing and the college years were waiting.

Chapter 8: The Recruiting Roller Coaster

Millions of kids grow up dreaming of earning an athletic scholarship to college. Unfortunately for the vast majority there just are not enough football scholarships to go around.

The 120 biggest name schools like Michigan, UCLA, and Alabama play in what the NCAA calls Football Bowl Subdivision (FBS) and in most cases are allowed eighty-five scholarships. Those must be full rides to include tuition, room and board, and books.

One step below FBS are the sixty-three schools in the Football Championship Subdivision (FCS). FCS schools are allowed sixty-five scholarships. A school can divvy those up, but no more than eighty-five players may receive football aid. Schools like Delaware, Northern Arizona, and North Dakota State make up this group.

The availability of scholarship money takes a sharp dive at lower levels. Division II schools like Grand Valley State, Northwest Missouri, and Minnesota Duluth are allowed thirty-six scholarships each. The scholarships may be broken up and portions may be doled out to an unlimited number of athletes. Most rosters have about one hundred players. Very few, if any, players get everything covered. There are approximately 150 DII schools. Some conferences restrict their scholarship number to as few as twenty-four.

The 239 schools that play in Division III (Mount Union, Hope, Wisconsin Whitewater) do not award any athletic scholarships. The ninety-two or so small schools that compete within the NAIA are each allowed twenty-four scholarships.

In reality, any football player who earns a partial football scholarship is lucky, considering how few there are compared to the number of athletes playing the sport.

It became evident right away that Jared would have a pretty good shot at a partial scholarship by the number of schools who were showing interest in him. The road to signing a national letter of intent to receive a scholarship would be a bumpy one, full of high hopes and disappointments.

It would be easy for the casual football fan to assume that recruiting for someone like Jared, an instant starter in the NFL, would be right out of a Hollywood movie like *The Blind Side*. The revolving door of big-name college coaches watching high school practices, making home visits, and cutting playful deals with little brothers does happen all of the time. It just never happened for Jared.

No coaches from any college ever visited the Veldheer's home.

Rejection is tough. Many times in recruiting, a young man gets cast off by a university's staff like a substandard cut of meat. One such experience came in the early summer of 2004, during a five hundred mile round-trip visit to Purdue University.

After an encouraging invite from a Boilermaker assistant coach, Jared and his dad headed for West

Lafayette, Indiana. The coaches asked Jared to do agility drills, a vertical jump test, and a timed forty-yard dash. The Veldheers were asked to wait while the coaches discussed what they had seen in Jared. An hour later they were sent on their way back to Michigan with a "Thanks, but no thanks."

What could have been taken as a crushing blow to a young man's hopes became a lesson in not letting the word "no" derail you.

The trip to Purdue wasn't a total loss for Jared. The Veldheers stopped in South Bend on their way home and met with Notre Dame's offensive line coach who had shown some interest. The visit led to Jared participating at the Notre Dame football camp, where he competed well against the other hopefuls assembled. Jared and his family were excited about him possibly playing for the Fighting Irish. The camp performance led to a family invitation to a Notre Dame game in the fall. The game day experience of touring the beautiful campus, the religious sanctity, and the tremendous academic offerings easily convinced Jared that if offered a chance to play for the Irish, he would say "Yes, I will."

From the disappointing lows of the Purdue visit to the excitement of being courted by one of college football's legendary programs, Jared and the Veldhees were learning that being recruited was similar to riding a rollercoaster. Right now, they were riding high and a Division 1 offer was looking imminent. That all changed when Notre Dame fired its coaching staff after the season. Unfortunately, Jared was a complete unknown to the replacements and didn't hear any further from Notre Dame.

But there was still another big-time scholarship offer possibility out there for Jared. Michigan State was by far the major college that had expressed the most interest in him, even more than Notre Dame. Jared got to experience the campus atmosphere through handful of basketball games at the raucous Breslin Center during his junior year, and he was on the sidelines for a couple of Spartan football games his senior year.

Jared's big thrill in East Lansing came when the lifelong basketball fan got to stand in front of 75,000 fans in Spartan Stadium and have his picture taken with one of his idols, MSU basketball coach Tom Izzo. That picture, proudly by Mary, still hangs in the Veldheer's family room.

The most vivid memory of the Michigan State recruiting process for Jim came when Jared's friend Joe Cawood stated prophetically while on the sideline in East Lansing, "You know, Jared could play in the NFL someday."

Little did anyone on the Spartan Stadium sideline know just how right Joe would be.

Michigan State's facilities were some of the best Jared would see during the whole recruiting process. Another positive was that East Lansing was a Big Ten school close to home. Becoming a Spartan was definitely something Jared would welcome if the opportunity were to present itself.

Unlike Purdue's flat "no" and the firing of the staff at Notre Dame, rejection would come from East Lansing in a different form. Sometimes silence can be crushing, and by the time December rolled around, Jared was hearing nothing from MSU.

The University of Michigan would show a passing interest in Jared as he was invited to a lineman one-day camp run by then head coach Lloyd Carr himself. Carr was far more encouraging and personable than Purdue's Tiller, but that was where the conversation with the Wolverine staff would end.

The leads on playing at the elite level of college football had all run dry. For many young men, this is the point where they bag the whole dream. Jared's hopes had soared with attention coming from four prestigious programs and had crashed on four separate occasions. Jared pressed on.

Luckily for Jared and the Veldheers, the recruiting roller coaster was about to end. Jared was about to discover something bigger than anything listed in a scholarship package—the right fit.

Chapter 9: Hello Hillsdale College

Sometime during the late Fall of 2004 at tiny Hillsdale College, basketball coach Ed Douma walked into football coach Keith Otterbein's office and said, "There is a 6' 8" kid over in Grand Rapids you need to take a look at."

Coach Douma knew Jared because Jared's big brother Aaron had recently completed his career playing basketball for Douma and the Chargers. He knew the kind of athlete Jared was. Jared had interest in playing both football or basketball in college and Douma saw a lot of unrefined athletic ability in the kid from Forest Hills Northern.

When asked what prompted Otterbein to follow up on Veldheer, he said the fact that Jared and the family already had ties to Hillsdale had played a big role.

"You always love it," the former Hillsdale football

player turned coach would explain. "When you don't have to spend all of your time selling the kid on your institution, it is easy to take a hard look at someone who understands the kind of place we are, and wants to be here."

Hillsdale definitely is unique when it comes to Division II football. It has one of the smallest enrollments at that level and some of the toughest academic standards as well. At many schools coaches are able to obtain an admissions waiver that allows certain athletes special admittance to the college or university. These incoming athletes' grades and test scores may be below what is acceptable to the common applicant, but because they may help an athletic program they are given the chance to show they can handle the load in the classroom as well.

No such waiver system exists at Hillsdale. President Larry Arnn has always refuted such a notion. Dr. Arnn, along with athletic director Don Brubacher, share a vision for building a program that can be an example of how a school can field teams of the highest caliber while still expecting academic excellence from its athletes.

Dr. Arnn once remarked at a Hillsdale football banquet, "We like Division II because it is about having a balance between athletics and life. It is a balance, not a compromise. We don't compromise our academic or athletic expectations here."

Hillsdale is uncompromising in more than how it treats its student-athletes. The college refuses all federal and state government money. This includes direct funding from the federal government as well as indirect funding in the form of financial aid students may receive through government grants and loans. This refusal of funding means Hillsdale is exempt from all legislation that regulates education in America.

One knee-jerk reaction is to accuse Hillsdale of simply not wanting to play by the rules that are designed to prevent discrimination and insure equal opportunity. All Hillsdale has to do in response is point to its more than 170 years of operating via the principles outlined in the U.S. Constitution and its leadership in providing equal opportunity before the laws were even enacted.

Hillsdale was the first college in America to specifically forbid in its charter any discrimination based on race, religion, or gender. It was the first college in Michigan and the second in the United States to admit women under the same criteria as men. Hillsdale was also one of very few colleges admitting African American students in 1844 when it was founded. During the Civil War, Hillsdale had a higher percentage of its male students enlist in the Union Army than any other non-military school.

Jared felt at home on the small campus ever since Aaron decided to attend. He had been in and out of all of the athletic facilities and had seen the complete overhaul of the academic buildings as well. These would open just in time for Jared to begin pursuing his interests in biology and the pre-med program, a huge positive for Jared and his family. Remember, athletics had always been something Jared did as one of the guys. Learning how stuff worked was Jared's bigger drive and really his number one priority for selecting a college. Hillsdale had some great faculty ready to show Jared how things in the world worked.

On a wintery night in early 2005, Coach Otterbein drove up to Grand Rapids to watch Jared play basketball. After another Husky win, he talked briefly with Jim and Mary and asked if he could have a word with Jared. After a few pleasantries "Otter" as he was known amongst the Hillsdale faithful, cut to the chase and offered Jared an athletic scholarship to play football at Hillsdale College.

Jared accepted the offer on the spot, and became Hillsdale's first verbal commitment for the 2005 recruiting class, a recruiting class that would be arguably one of its best in the last twenty years. The scholarship wouldn't become official until National Signing Day in early February, but for Jared there was instant relief.

There would be no more of the ups and downs of schools showing great interest and then falling quiet. There would be no more taking long trips for visits and there would be no more having to leave his basketball teammates on Saturday morning practices to go through some kind of meat market testing at schools he knew deep down he really had no interest in attending.

Going to Hillsdale also presented the unique possibility that Jared could explore joining the basketball team once football finished each fall. He wasn't going to be able to do that at Notre Dame or any of the other big schools.

Hillsdale College and its tight-knit community would prove to be a great place for Jared grow athletically, meet his future wife Morgan, and excel in the classroom.

Chapter 10: Aha

How freshmen football players handle the first few weeks of their college experience can be a huge determinant in the success of their college careers.

Many are away from home for the first time. Many have been the dominate "big fish in a small pond" their whole lives. When they show up as a freshman the slate gets washed clean and every seventeen or eighteen-year-old has to begin writing life's next chapter as an athlete, a student, and ultimately as a man.

That can be a daunting feeling even at a small school like Hillsdale. It can be so daunting that some players don't even make it through the first night, packing up and heading home before bed check. Some guys last a week or so. Some might stick it out until Christmas. The majority do make it, learning how to balance the challenge of college football as well as the rigors of one of the top liberal arts schools in the country. The athletic department and college offer a number of support systems and most freshmen find that once the growing pains subside. Each student can find a niche and begin to embrace the opportunities over the course of the next few years.

For Jared it was pretty easy—a lot like that day camp when Mary gave him his last chance to not go. Jared had been able to handle these types of situations with a strong sense of self. Once at Hillsdale, Jared absolutely thrived in the environment, relying on those core attributes that had already made him successful at the high school level.

He was challenged daily in the classroom and began forging life-long friendships with young men and women who shared a lot of the same character traits. He was also receiving some of the best football coaching of his career from Hillsdale offensive line coach Nate Shreffler.

It's not that Coach Brent Myers and staff hadn't provided good coaching at Forest Hills Northern, doing all they could to field a winning team. It is just uncommon for high school coaches to have the time and manpower to provide the same environment an athlete gets at the collegiate level. This goes for strength training, conditioning, as well as technique.

The interesting connection for Jared was that Myers and Shreffler had been teammates at Hillsdale in the early 1990s and had won the school's last league title thirteen years earlier in '92.

For Jared, there were things like size and speed that immediately put him out in front of the other incoming freshmen, but there were areas like footwork where many of the other players were significantly ahead. Still, it was obvious to his teammates that this big kid had some serious potential.

Schuyler File was a defensive lineman who would become a close friend of Jared's. He said, "I remember testing right when we started camp as freshmen. Jared was around 6' 7 1/2" and probably weighed 255. He ran the 110-yard sprints like a deer, faster than any other o-lineman. We get to the bench press and I think he maxed out at 250 or 255. I thought to myself here is this guy who has not grown into his body yet. He's going to be scary good if he does."

On the field Jared became a technician of proper blocking footwork. This had been one of the big knocks on him as a Division I recruit.

He said, "I would go to these camps at the big colleges and I was basically trying to use my basketball defensive stance with my feet and I guess it didn't impress them much."

Under the watchful eye of Shreffler the footwork came together fairly early in the learning process. Hillsdale's offense and blocking schemes also made sense to Jared quickly. Although he was definitely improving, the Hillsdale staff decided early on that they would redshirt the freshman and give him time to grow into that body.

Redshirting essentially resets the clock for players who don't participate in games throughout the season. They still practice, participate in team activities, and at Hillsdale at least dress with everyone else for home games. They retain that year of eligibility and have four more years to compete.

Shreffler and Otterbein figured he would be far more beneficial to the program as a polished fifth-year senior than as a green rookie just out of high school. Jared saw the logic in this and had always believed in his coaches.

Some athletes don't handle being red-shirted very well, taking it as wasted year. Jim Veldheer sheds some light on how Jared handled the situation, "Getting red-shirted is another one of those adjustments that college athletes have to handle. For some it is a slap in the face. A lot of recruits have never stood on the sidelines, ever. They were called up to the varsity as high school freshmen or sophomores and starred in every game they had ever played. Jared handled it just like he did when he was hardly playing his freshman year in high school or when he was sitting during FHN's district championship game in basketball. It was what Coach Otterbein and his staff thought was best for the program and Jared accepted that. He actually did more than accept it. He embraced it."

During that season Jared took advantage not only of Shreffler's tutelage on the field, but also in the weight room where the line coach was also the strength and conditioning coordinator. Jared loved having a college weight room that he could utilize to not only build strength and muscle but also to increase his speed and mobility. Gains were immediate through not only determination and work ethic but through his typical scientific approach to everything. Constantly analyzing the exercises, Jared was doing and tweaking them for increased performance. Jared also combined the physical workouts with the careful attention he had developed toward his diet and had a tremendous first semester of growth at Hillsdale College.

Still a difficult decision loomed. Would Jared play for Coach Douma on the Hillsdale basketball team? He had struggled with the question during the entire football season. He knew that if he played basketball, he would lose weight from the running. During his senior year of high school Jared lost twenty pounds during the basketball season. On the other hand, he loved the game. He could play with his high school teammate and current roommate

Travis Worst, and he knew deep inside that his dad and brother were hoping he would continue to play.

In the end Jared concluded that basketball training would be counter-productive to the development he gained during football season. He also felt loyal to Coach Otterbein, his teammates, and the football staff for giving him the opportunity and scholarship to play football at Hillsdale College. Jared would focus on football with laser precision.

No one can really pinpoint it, not even Jared, his aha moment. Many people from his father, to Coach Otterbein, and his good friend Mark Ehnis will tell you that there was an obvious epiphany in Jared that first fall away from home. Call it an aha moment. It was a moment when this eighteen-year-old realized just how big and how good of a football player he might become by the time his days at Hillsdale College were finished.

"It was like a light bulb," Otterbein tells. "It's like he suddenly realized, 'Hey, I can get as big as these guys playing on Sunday. I can get that strong and as quick.' We never talked about the NFL really, but his drive and work ethic kicked into another gear, and he would be a great leader for us in that sense over the course of the next four years."

When he returned home at Christmas break, Jared's dad noticed a huge change during a pickup basketball game. Jim noted, "At 6' 5 " I have guarded a number of players posting up on the block near the basket. My goal as a defender is to deny the pass into the post by defending either on the high side or the low side of the player, depending on where the ball is on the court. That night in December when I tried to move from one side to the other on Jared I found it impossible. He was so wide and so strong that he could hold me off on one side, catch the pass on the other side, and make a move for an easy basket. If I played directly behind him he would use a drop step move with his legs and shoulders that would catapult me into the bleachers. Jared was nearing 300 pounds at this time, and I still thought that he would be a great addition to a college basketball program as a low-post, immovable force."

Mark Ehnis, who had been friends with Jared since fourth grade, noticed a change as well but on a completely different plane.

"The physical differences were obvious but it was this aggressiveness in Jared that I had never seen. He was always just the big, nice kid, kind of chubby at times, everybody loved him. He didn't have any kind of mean streak at all. I grew up with a twin brother so we were always aggressive and tried to get Jared to be a little more aggressive. When he came home that Christmas break from Hillsdale, he had finally found that aggressiveness. He was still a great guy, but when we would lift or play basketball he had a completely different attitude."

That 2005 red-shirt year would be the last season Jared would spend absent from football team's starting lineup. Jared wasn't the only player making immense progress either and the fortunes of the Hillsdale program were about to achieve new heights.

Chapter 11: Belief without Evidence

Keith Otterbein was beginning his sixth season in Hillsdale in 2006, and had so far delivered Charger fans three straight years of 4-7 and back-to-back years of 5-6. An All-American linebacker at Hillsdale, Coach Otterbein became a hall of fame head coach at Hillsdale's rival Ferris State. When Otterbein returned to Hillsdale, he wanted to restore the proud tradition of great football that the college had delivered to fans for over one hundred years. Some of the college's big name players include Coach Muddy Waters and Chester Marcol, 1972 NFC Rookie of the Year and kicker for Green Bay Packers.

So far, things had not gone well for Otterbein. In fact things had not gone well for Otterbein since leaving Ferris State in 1995 to become an assistant at Division I Ball State. After going 7-4 in his first season as the running backs coach in Muncie, the Cardinals reeled off eight straight wins the next season to earn a berth in the Las Vegas Bowl. After that, things kind of dried up win-wise at Ball State. The next four years, Ball State was 5-6, 1-10, 0-11, and 5-6 before Otterbein made the move back to Hillsdale.

When asked how he managed to endure that stretch of losing at Ball State followed by losing seasons in his early years at Hillsdale, Otterbein credits undying faith. By sticking with the core values you know, you will eventually become successful. "Staying in the game" one might say.

"It's belief without evidence," Otterbein declares. "You just have to stick to your principles and keep doing what you know in your heart works and you just keep plugging along knowing you are improving even if it's not showing up on the football field. All of those basic principles I learned from Coach Dick Lowry when I was an assistant here at Hillsdale. I continued to learn as an assistant at Central Michigan, which led to the success we had at Ferris. I knew it would eventually all pay off."

Otter credits that same "belief without evidence" as

the core buy-in that would eventually allow Jared and his teammates to bring some of the glory back to Hillsdale College Football.

"That whole group, and even the kids when I first got here, all believed in what we were doing and that by continuing to do the little things," Otterbein explains, "we would be successful."

2006 would prove to be another year of "belief without evidence" with Hillsdale being stuck in mediocrity and another 5-6 season. It however would be an invaluable year of growth for the players and the program that was about to make a big splash in the Great Lakes Intercollegiate Athletic Conference.

Jared had worked himself into a starting position during spring and fall practices. In 2006, for the next forty-six games, Jared was the only starting left tackle for Hillsdale College. Gaining strength and agility, studying the offense, and improving technique, Jared became, literally, an immovable object on the Hillsdale offensive line. He would yield zero sacks over the course of his college career, a stat very few linemen can claim at any level.

Chapter 12: The Tipping Point

During the summer of 2007, the Hillsdale College coaching staff would do some major "under the hood" tweaking of its offense, and what better speed shop to take it to than the headquarters of the recent Super Bowl champs, the Indianapolis Colts.

The relationship with the Colts was multi-faceted. Hillsdale's quarterback Mark Nicolet and his father were friends with the previous head coach Tony Dungy. Coach Dungy knew of Hillsdale because he grew up in a town not far from there called Jackson. The final piece of the puzzle that summer would be bringing the Colts offensive line coach and former NFL All Pro lineman Howard Mudd back into the Hillsdale fold. Mudd had started at Hillsdale in the 1960s, gone on to be an excellent pro player and coach, but he hadn't had much contact or involvement with Hillsdale since his college days.

By the end of the summer, Hillsdale's old vanilla pro-set offense would develop its own new flavor.

Even though many of the base plays remained the same, Hillsdale was now a hurry-up, no-huddle offense, just like the one Peyton Manning had driven to the podium picking up the Lombardi Trophy as Super Bowl Champs. With Nicolet as a 4th year starter, he was more than capable of directing the offense from the field.

Hillsdale started the 2007 season on fire. Never before had Hillsdale started a season by scoring forty or more points in each of its first three games. Any fan who hadn't noticed the new-look Chargers yet definitely would after the team dismantled Ashland at Hillsdale's Homecoming during week three of the football season. The Eagles would eventually make the NCAA Division II playoffs that year, but not before having their hats handed to them 49-28 by Hillsdale in front of a happy homecoming crowd. It was a game that could have been a lot worse for Ashland had Otter not called off the team midway through the second half.

Mark Nicolet would set a new Hillsdale single game record with 426 passing yards and he didn't even play the whole game.

One of Jared's closest friends, and a member of the same recruiting class, Aaron Waldie, would finish the day eleven receiving yards shy of Hillsdale's single game record.

Not only was the Hillsdale offense doing something it had never done, Jared was doing something he had never done. Over the course of spring practice and then into the fall, the big lineman had discovered a punch technique and it was driving his opponents nuts. Now, this is not a closed fist punch like a boxer would throw, but one with an open palm. Most of those opponents were Hillsdale's own defensive linemen that he would face in practice, and because of Jared's height, most of those blows were landing right in the earhole or the facemask.

It got so bad in practice for the defense that defensive line coach Aaron Shreffler finally pulled his whole position group aside and told them bluntly, "Look. He is going to hit you right in the face. Do something about it."

The other technique Jared perfected that season was blocking with just one arm.

As Hillsdale's offensive line coach Nate Shreffler explains, "You are longer and have longer reach with one arm than two. Jared is so strong that he can start the block with one arm and then once he gets you going where he wants you to go, he'll engage the other arm or throw that nasty punch."

Hillsdale's 8-3 final record would be good enough for a third place finish in the GLIAC. Not only was it the Chargers' first winning season in eight years, it was record setting on many fronts.

Mark Nicolet's 3,145 passing yards were a new GLIAC single-season record that earned him league player of the year.

Jared and his veteran offensive line could claim at least a small portion of that honor. In near anonymity, they had provided the backbone for an offense that literally had come out of nowhere.

Five Chargers would earn All-GLIAC first team honors. Jared would receive his first recognition as a

Charger by being picked All-GLIAC second team.

Chapter 13: Glancing the Future

As Mark Nicolet lit up Division II football week after week as quarterback that fall, professional scouts began to take notice. For the first time in a decade, scouts were stopping by Muddy Waters Stadium to catch practice or watch tape of this quarterback who had burst upon the scene. This would pay huge dividends for Jared and a number of other players for years to come.

As scouts watched Nicolet, they also became intrigued with linebacker Tom Korte, receiver Aaron Waldie, and this young skyscraper named Jared Veldheer playing left tackle.

The possibilities of Jared becoming a professional football player were beginning to take shape. None of this was lost on teammate and close friend Schuyler File.

In an interview, File described his own realization of

Veldheer's future potential, "This was the time when I started thinking Jared had a legitimate shot at playing at the next level. He was over 300 pounds and was starting to really become an elite athlete. That Christmas Break we went to the Orange Bowl to watch Virginia Tech and Kansas. People would come up to us and ask if Jared played for the Dolphins or some other NFL team. The funny thing is he still had two more years of ball at Hillsdale."

Jared's name was beginning to move beyond family and the Hillsdale fan-base. He landed on the national Division II football scene. During the summer of 2008, he was named a preseason All-American by The Sporting News and D2football.com. It was hard to believe this was the same kid who hadn't started on his high school varsity football team until halfway through his junior year. Five years later he was being picked as one of the best in the country at the D2 level.

Although Jared won't admit to thinking much about the NFL in 2008, that offseason he asked Coach Shreffler one day about how he compared to other linemen from the GLIAC who had been fifth and sixth round picks in the 2005 draft. Jared asked to see some tape on both so he could compare his play to players who had just completed their third NFL seasons. Shreffler said he would do some digging and then get back to Jared.

"After watching the tapes myself," Shreffler recalls, "I told Jared I wasn't going to let him see them. He kind of looked at me weird and I told him that I thought he was already better than both of those guys as seniors and he was only going into his junior year."

It was tempting to dream about a professional football career but Jared, Aaron Waldie, Tom Korte, and every other player on the team knew the most important task at hand was to focus on preparing for the 2008 Hillsdale Football season.

Chapter 14: Putting in Work

The 2008 Chargers would finish the year at 7-4. The back-to-back winning seasons were the first in twelve years. Despite some disappointing moments after the 8-3 of 2007, Jared and the team still continued to improve. This player development, and a few hard lessons along the way, would prove invaluable down the road.

Homecoming of that season would be a breakout performance for Jared from an individual standpoint. He had established himself as a very good player. The way Jared dominated any opponent the Findlay Oilers sent his way was unforgettable. By the end of the third quarter, Oiler defenders were drawing straws on the sidelines to see who was going to face Jared.

They say if you notice an offensive lineman, it is usually because he keeps jumping offsides or getting flagged for holding. That wasn't the case on that October day in Hillsdale. Veldheer's dominance on the left side of the line was becoming as big a part of the show as any of the so-called "skill positions." It was hard for fans to take their eyes off him from the minute this giant walked out for the coin flip until his last play from the line of scrimmage.

Although Jared had a great day, Hillsdale still struggled at times to execute its offense against a team that had won one game all year. This got fans' tummies trembling as they thought of the monumental task lying ahead of them in seven days. The Chargers were headed to Grand Valley to face the #1 ranked Lakers, the most dominant program in all of Division II football.

The fears were definitely warranted, and Grand Valley whipped Hillsdale 41-10.

As coach Otterbein gathered his dejected players around him that night, each was faced with a choice, a decision to make. They, too, could dwell on the defeat or they could flush it and resolve to continue improving.

They had faced one of the all-time great Division II

football teams, riding a national-record regular season winning streak. If Hillsdale had aspirations of truly becoming an elite program, Grand Valley had just given Hillsdale a demonstration of the level of play necessary for such a distinction. The lesson would not be lost on Jared or any of the Hillsdale players.

Hillsdale wouldn't face another program like Grand Valley for 364 more days, but the sting of the 41-10 defeat would propel them daily. It became bulletin board material; their drive was focused.

For Jared, 2008 was now his 3rd consecutive season of not yielding a sack. He had established himself as the best left tackle in the GLIAC and one of the very best in the country. Jared would be named first team All-GLIAC and All-Region. His biggest accolade would come though when D2football.com named him to its All-American Team, considered to be one of the most well-researched and prestigious of the division's All-American teams.

Tom Korte would sign with the Pittsburgh Steelers as an undrafted free-agent linebacker. Aaron Waldie would set a new Hillsdale record for career touchdown receptions and get a look with Saskatchewan of the Canadian Football League. Neither would make their teams' final rosters but the Veldheers followed the journey of each closely in anticipation of Jared getting a shot at professional football within the coming year.

Chapter 15: Going Viral...the First Time

The buffet trays had barely been cleared from the 2008 Hillsdale College Football Banquet when preparation for the 2009 season began. In less than 24 hours after their banquet, Jared and the Chargers were in a full lather preparing for their last season together and each felt they still had a lot to accomplish.

Day after day, preparations continued right up to the start of spring break. Before any of the Chargers could escape campus for the beach, they would be tested in exercises similar to those at the NFL Draft Combine. What Jared would learn from his spring testing numbers was that his "measurables" were as good as any tackle in the country. His speed, fitness, and agility were not only in the upper echelon of college linemen, but were as good or better than most offensive tackles about to be drafted by NFL clubs.

Those numbers were great news to the Veldheers, Hillsdale coaches, and inquiring scouts. They're just not the kind of thing that causes the average fan to take notice. These days it takes a viral video on YouTube.

Thousands and thousands of web viewers would get their first glimpse of the raw power and brute strength of Jared Veldheer via a clip Jared's dad shot during the annual fundraising liftathon.

Jared's 425 pound hang-clean, a lift where an athlete starts with the weight resting above the knees, lifts and snaps underneath it before standing with the bar resting on the upper chest, was nearly superhuman to watch. Jim's uploaded YouTube video would get over one hundred thousand hits.

Word of this "monster" at tiny Hillsdale had already begun to spread through the small college football and NFL Draft Internet message boards, but those twenty seconds of Internet video really solidified the buzz. Jared had gone viral.

The buzz only got louder when a New York Jets scout showed up at Hillsdale for the NFL's "junior pro-day" to time Jared and a few Chargers in the forty-yard dash and take a few other measurables. On that cool March day, Jared ran a 4.87, a time faster than any tackle drafted that year. The 4.87 forty run by Jared landed him on every NFL teams radar.

YouTube videos are great, but what NFL teams like a lot more are measurables. No tackle with NFL size who runs a 4.87 is going to go unnoticed. All of the attention would keep Jared very busy for the next twelve months.

Chapter 16: Eleven-Fourteen

"Eleven-fourteen."

If you had stopped by a Hillsdale College practice during the spring and fall of 2009, you would have heard that odd combination of numbers a lot.

"That's what this is all about boys, eleven-fourteen."

"We won't make eleven-fourteen playing like this."

When the team finished each session of preseason camp, all 100 plus players gathered in a giant huddle and on the count of three shouted, "Eleven-fourteen."

In fact, "eleven-fourteen" became such a part of the vernacular that to even enter the Hillsdale College football locker room on off-hours, players keyed in the digits 1-1-1-4.

"Eleven-fourteen, November 14, 2009, was the opening round of the Division II playoffs," explained quarterback Troy Weatherhead. "It was Jared as a captain who really pushed that as one of our team goals. We are always trying to win the GLIAC conference, but we wanted to do something no other team had ever done at Hillsdale, earn a D2 playoff bid."

With high expectations for themselves and a historic goal firmly in front of them, the first couple of weeks of early practice were ladened with internal battles between the offense and the defense and between players fighting it out for the last remaining starting spots.

As all of that was being sorted out on the inside, there were plenty of doubts surrounding the program on the outside. The talk surrounded replacing record-setting receiver Aaron Waldie and linebacker Tom Korte. There were even questions about whether Troy Weatherhead was right for the job.

No matter what questions were raised from the outside, or when things didn't quite click on a play in practice, it was Jared who would often calm everyone's nerves with one simple command.

"Flush it," he would repeat over and over again through spring practice and fall camp.

"I can't tell you how many times I heard Jared say that," Weatherhead recalls. "All I had to do was manage the offense. Jared did the rest, leading by example and keeping everybody focused."

For Jared there was an additional preseason detail to add to his game. NFL scouts began to tell him through the Hillsdale staff that for a small college player to be considered legitimate, teams needed to see an additional level of dominance. On film he had to be a mauler, and Jared's first chance to show that would come against the Pumas of St. Joe's College.

After a convincing 37-7 opening week victory for the Chargers, Hillsdale line coach Nate Shreffler pulled Jared aside to help him refine his "mauling." Veldheer had physically beaten up everyone he faced on the St. Joe's team, sometimes with moves resembling mixed martial arts and professional wrestling.

"He was just so much bigger and physically stronger

that he was throwing guys," Shreffler recalls. "I just told him that he can drive guys into the ground, get lots of knock downs, but to be careful so his physical play didn't get misconstrued as dirty."

The next five weeks Hillsdale dominated opponents, squeaked out wins, and dropped a pair of stinkers.

One loss on the résumé in Division II will get you into the field of twenty-four playoff teams. Two losses will put you right on the in-or-out bubble. A third loss means doom.

Eleven-Fourteen was still possible but Hillsdale needed to peel off wins in its final five games to even have a shot at the playoff invite.

To most fans, playoff hopes were already doomed; next up on the schedule was the Grand Valley Lakers.

When Grand Valley came to Hillsdale on October 10th of 2009, the Lakers were ranked #1 in Division II and riding a forty-eight game regular season unbeaten streak. The program had not lost a conference game in five seasons. Grand Valley was averaging more than fifty points a game over the course of the previous two weeks and the inferior opponent Findlay had just blown out Hillsdale.

"All week long," quarterback Troy Weatherhead recalls, "we had one great practice after another. Like Jared always would tell us, we just had to flush that Findlay game out of our system and take our shot at Grand Valley."

That is exactly what Hillsdale did. On a beautiful homecoming weekend, Hillsdale stood toe to toe with the four-time National Champions and led 17-15 at Halftime.

The Lakers would regain the lead at 24-20 before Hillsdale got its hands on the ball one last time. There were five minutes and nineteen seconds left in the fourth quarter and the Chargers would use almost all of them.

Having started at its own 33, Weatherhead had the Chargers in Grand Valley territory in just two plays. In complete control of the offense and the game, the junior signal caller would methodically take almost four minutes to go the next fifty yards. With 1:30 left on the clock, speedster Mike Blanchard made a spectacular catch, stepping out at the Laker one-yard line. After Vinnie Panizzi came up empty on first and goal, short yardage specialist Billy Kanitz found some room to the left of center behind the surge of Jared and guard DJ Loy for the go-ahead touchdown with 36 seconds left to play. As the heap of bodies untangled in the end zone, celebrations were already beginning to break out around Muddy Waters Stadium. Mark Petro's extra point was good to make the score Hillsdale 27, Grand Valley 24 with a minute and change left in regulation.

Grand Valley, and its forty-eight game win streak, wasn't dead yet. The team would start its final possession on its own 22-yard line. With precision, the Lakers picked their way to the Hillsdale 32 to set up a 49-yard field goal attempt, hoping to force overtime with a handful of ticks left on the clock.

As local cable and webcast play-by-play announcer Jim Measle described it, "The kick has plenty of leg but it's wide right. Hillsdale wins. Hillsdale has just beaten the number one team in the nation."

Seemingly before the ball had even hit the ground, a stream of Hillsdale fans stormed the turf at Muddy Waters Stadium and mobbed the Charger team. It was a scene like no other.

The dream of Eleven-Fourteen remained alive.

Nothing was certain, and two-loss teams are left on the outside of the playoff looking in every year. Hillsdale and Jared did what they could by looking even sharper in each of their remaining four weeks.

In their last home game, and possibly last game together, Jared and the rest of the Chargers blasted Tiffin 59-24.

The offensive line and senior Vinnie Panizzi put together the biggest rushing day per carry of their careers. They gained 128 yards on seventeen attempts while scoring five touchdowns, all in the first half as the Chargers took a 49-7 lead to the locker room at the break.

The starters had their pads off by the third quarter, and Hillsdale cruised most of the day. The 9-2 regular season finish was the best showing by the program since 1992.

Within twenty-four hours, Hillsdale would know if it had done something even the 1992 Chargers had not done, qualified for the Division II playoffs. It was all in the hands of the NCAA regional selection committee.

As is tradition at Hillsdale College, football coaches, support staff, fans, players, and their families gather on the Sunday after the final regular season game to honor the senior class and hand out end of the year awards.

Midway through the senior speeches, Hillsdale sports information director Brad Monastiere slipped coach Otterbein a note. Everyone in the arena saw the exchange and there was a palpable gasp as the Chargers' coach approached the microphone.

"I have before me the Super Region 3 playoff seedings. Number one: Minnesota Duluth, Number two: Grand Valley. Both of those teams have byes. Number three: Minnesota State Mankato. Number four: Nebraska Kearney. Number five: Saginaw Valley," Otterbein paused and finally, just slightly, cracked the poker face he had been wearing since peeking at the note. "And at number six...Hillsdale College."

With those words, the arena erupted. Receiver AJ Kegg, seated at the senior table jumped to his feet and the rest of the crowd followed. Nineteen years after making the switch from NAIA, Hillsdale had finally earned its first Division II playoff berth. The win over Grand Valley had sent the Hillsdale name in shockwaves across the national landscape. Reaching the playoffs sent out a whole different message of legitimacy for a program that had been trying to return to national relevance since the late 1980s.

"The emotion in that gym was incredible," Troy Weatherhead recalls. "The parents and families were cheering as if we had just scored the go ahead touchdown against GV. Some were crying, others in shock. It was one of the greatest moments I have ever been a part of."

Hillsdale opened the playoffs on the road at Minnesota State Mankato with a thrilling 27-24 overtime win. The team returned to town with a police escort and jubilant fans lining campus streets.

The excitement carried over the next week as fans from all over Michigan and the Midwest flocked to Grand Valley's Lubbers Stadium for the second round and a rematch with the Lakers. Sadly for the Hillsdale fans, Jared, and his teammates, Grand Valley would get its revenge with a lopsided win.

Even though Hillsdale never really contended all afternoon, the Chargers left the field the same way they had entered, to a standing ovation and loud cheer of thanks from all of their fans. The ovation wasn't for what had transpired over the course of the previous two hours and forty-two minutes, it was for all that had transpired over the course of the past four years, an astounding amount of progress.

Every player had bought into Otterbein's system and philosophy, and the program was in good hands. Because so many had "stayed in the game" through 5-6 seasons and grueling physical conditioning, a return to the playoffs and an outright-GLIAC championship would come to the program in the following seasons.

Jared had played a huge role in laying the groundwork and rebuilding the foundation. Now, his work as a college athlete was complete.

Photos

Jared, six months, twenty-four pounds

Jared in the Forest Hills Youth Football League and as a 9th grader at
Forest Hills Northern High School

NAME __JARED VELDHEER__

SEASON __1996__

AGE __9__

HOMETOWN __GRAND RAPIDSS__

HEIGHT __5'00"__ WEIGHT __104__

POSITION __3RD BASE__

TEAM __MERRILL LYNCH__

LEAGUE __WESTERN__

COACH __EDSENGA__

Jared's first and only (at time of printing this book) trading card

Mary, Jared, Meghan, and Jim Veldheer at Hillsdale College

At Hillsdale, Jared was often literally head and shoulders above the competition.

Jared with Hillsdale president Larry Arnn, author Andy Losik and daughter Kasey, and head coach Keith Otterbein

As a two-year captain, Jared leads Hillsdale onto the field.

Jim, Jared, and Aaron Veldheer after Hillsdale's monumental upset over Grand Valley State University.

Jared with coaching legend Howard Schnellenberger at the Texas Vs. The Nation game in El Paso.

Size of school didn't matter in El Paso as Jared performed well against players from all divisions.

Jared with <u>D2Football.com</u>'s Josh Buchanan. Preseason All-American status on the highly regarded website firmly inserted Jared's name into the pro hopeful conversation.

Jared works out for NFL scouts at his Pro Day.

The Veldheer Family shortly after Jared was selected in the 3rd Round of the NFL Draft by the Oakland Raiders.

Jared's nephew may have been one of the littlest Raider fans but he was mighty proud of his great big uncle.

Jared's sister Meghan wearing Raider legend Cliff Branch's three Super Bowl rings during a Thanksgiving game at AT&T Stadium against the Cowboys

Jared with Hillsdale and then Raider teammate Andre Holmes shortly after their Thanksgiving game against the Dallas Cowboys

Bay Area photographer Bob Carr produces Silver and Black Report
and highlighted many of Jared's successes in Oakland.

Michigan sports radio host Bill Simonson is a Veldheer family friend
and has mentored Jared on media relations.

Jared getting in a workout at PowerStrength, the training facility he co-founded with childhood friend Mark Ehnis

Jared speaking to students at his alma mater, Forest Hills Northern Middle School

Jared with Mark Ehnis (top) . Fun with young Raider fans (middle).
Teaming up with Michigan State record setter Alyssa DeHaan (bottom
left) and Dr. Ed. Kornoelje

Jared appeared in a Brann's Steakhouse and Grille commercial for the Michigan-based restaurant chain during the 2015-2016 season. So did brother and agent Aaron (just to Jared's left, looking up at his much bigger "little" brother).

Jared proposing to Morgan Podkul, a star athlete in her own right on Hillsdale's volleyball team

Jared signing his free-agent contract with the Arizona Cardinals, joined on the left by team president Michael Bidwill and on the right by his wife Morgan

Chapter 17: Finding the Right NFL Agent

One of the advantages that the smaller school pro prospects have over their big school athletes is the ability to sign with an agent earlier. The Division II season for most teams ends two weeks before Thanksgiving. With a bazillion bowl games played by any team with a winning record, Division I prospects often don't turn in their pads until deep into the holidays or, in some cases, well into the new year. Agents only sign so many clients, but the real jump the D2 guys get over the boys from Alabama and Southern Cal is in beginning their training for the upcoming NFL Scouting Combine and their senior pro days. These players will already be hard at work training while many big school players are still playing out bowl season.

The Veldheers, and especially Jared, had hoped to be done with the process as quickly as possible. Jim and Mary had been working all angles to help find the best representation for their son. Jared just wanted the process finished.

Sorting through this quagmire of over 750 registered agents started for Mr. and Mrs. Veldheer well before Jared's senior season at Hillsdale. The goal was to let Jared focus on football while his parents did the major legwork in attracting and evaluating agents.

Although Jared's measurables were raising eyebrows, the Veldheers weren't content to sit idle and have agents come to them. By the end of March, the family had begun a conversation with agent Joe Linta, whose most notable client at the time was Baltimore Ravens' QB Joe Flacco.

Linta told the Veldheers that Jared had the potential to be a third to fourth round pick, but it would take ten months of complete dedication to football to make that happen.

The Veldheers also left no stone unturned when it came to finding someone to help them best understand the draft process and discover what might put Jared in the best possible situation. Even though Hillsdale hadn't had a player drafted since 1980, it still had a couple of prominent alumni in the League.

Jim contacted Indianapolis Colts offensive line coach Howard Mudd late in the spring of 2009. Having helped the Hillsdale staff get things back on track a couple of years earlier, Mudd was now more than happy to help Jared in any way he could. After spending nearly an hour and a half on the phone, the Veldheers had found a mentor who had confirmed a lot of what Linta was telling them. Mudd got even more technical with what teams look for in regards to how well a player bent at the knees and played through the whistle.

Another Hillsdale grad who wields quite a bit of influence in the NFL is Denver Broncos executive Tom Heckert. In 2009, he was still the Philadelphia Eagles' GM and was able to field some of the Veldheers questions, especially the legal and procedural ones.

When Jared returned home after his junior year at Hillsdale, he and Jim hit the road, a lot like they had done five years earlier while looking at colleges. The stakes were arguably bigger now as they began to tour training facilities and get to know some of the potential strength and conditioning coaches who would be preparing him for the Combine in early 2010.

Athletes and families may talk to agents, interview them, tour facilities together, but per NCAA rules, they may not accept anything, not a cup of coffee, not a dinner, not a plane ticket to a meeting, nothing. That also prohibits an agent from providing compensation to any of the trainers who may put a potential client through a workout. This can be a significant financial burden on the athlete and his family during this unique courting process. Sure there is always the potential for a big payday in the end, but that money is at least a year away when the real shopping is happening the summer before a player's senior year.

The Veldheers traveled to facilities in Pittsburgh, Bradenton, Florida, and Chicago where the big lineman would participate in training sessions, often with established professional clients doing their offseason work. Jared enjoyed the workouts, but really had not invested much personally into the process of selecting the agent. Ultimately, that decision would be his, but luckily he had a mom and dad whom he trusted implicitly to handle the triaging of all potential representation.

As Preseason All-American honors began to roll in and the hype increased, so did Jared's focus on football in his senior year. The back and forth agent courting was all on Jim and Mary. They were prepared to help organize the Hillsdale football parents' booster club and to host the many agents who would travel that season to see Jared play at Hillsdale.

It might have seemed a little distracting for them as they tried to take in every play of their son's last college football season, but hosting these potential representatives gave them the unique opportunity to really size-up the person who could eventually become Jared's agent. For a parent, getting the right person to fill that role is huge because, in essence, Jim and Mary had always been Jared's agents. In a close-knit family like the Veldheers, they weren't going to just let anyone assume that important role.

As the season wore on and more agents flew up to Grand Rapids to meet the family or made their way to games on Saturday, Jim and Mary would find themselves liking many different agents for different reasons. Sometimes Jim would be drawn to some of the more glitzy guys, while Mary would find some other aspect of an agent really intriguing and end up being sold that he was the one for Jared.

Little did anyone know that as this played out through the summer and early fall of 2009, the seed that would eventually grow into Jared finding the right fit with the right agent had been planted by older brother Aaron back on November 6, 2008.

Aaron, an attorney in Chicago, had attended a seminar on sports marketing and player representation given by Rick Smith, a top NFL agent and the founder of Priority Sports and Entertainment. Jared was nearing the close of his junior season when Aaron attended this seminar. When the presentation concluded, Aaron approached Rick and told him that he had a huge little brother who some were starting to think might have a future in the League. There is no telling how many times Smith must hear that about somebody's brother. He told Aaron very politely, "If your brother is really good, they'll find him and he'll be in the NFL."

Smith and Priority's Director of Football Operations Mike McCartney began to send out feelers to their contacts in NFL scouting departments. With the feedback they received, it seemed that the Veldheer kid just might be good enough to make it and it might be worth Smith's time to consider having Priority Sports represent him.

Rick Smith had to see this kid play for himself. He called Aaron and asked him to drop a tape by the office. Smith and McCartney sat down and watched it together with Aaron.

After finally meeting Jim and Mary, Rick had forged a connection with the family. The Veldheers really liked Rick, and Priority Sports Entertainment became one of the highest firms on their list. All agreed that they would meet up to tour the Peyton Manning owned D1 Sports training facility in Nashville as soon as Jared's senior season ended.

When Hillsdale was finally eliminated from the D2 playoffs, it looked like the week following Thanksgiving was going to be a busy one, complete with a little time in the sun on South Beach and some NFL glitz.

Besides Smith and Priority Sports, there were still other agents in the mix, one being Peter Schaffer. Schaffer had arranged a weekend meeting in Miami for Jared to tour the training facility where he sent his players. The itinerary included some relaxation on South Beach capped with nice seats at Sunday night's Dolphins and Patriots' game.

A California company of agents had also extended an invite to meet and tour their facilities in the LA area if nothing definitive came from Nashville or Miami.

Now that Jared had completed his college eligibility, agents were permitted to begin picking up the cost of meals, travel, and all of the other niceties that are part of this courtship. Living the highlife on some power broker's dime didn't last long though for the Veldheers.

The Veldheers arrived in Nashville on a Wednesday night and had a pleasant dinner with Rick. The more time they spent together, the more they hit it off. For Jared, the real test would come in the morning.

After taking a quick spin through the facility, Jared met D1's head of training Kurt Hester and prepared for an NFL style workout.

Just like in Pittsburgh, Florida, and Chicago, Jared showed the D1 staff he could match the intensity and strength of NFL Players. Although he may have attended a small college whose strength coach was also his line coach, Jared had the raw talent to take it to the next level. Thirteen-year NFL left tackle and All-Pro selection Brad Hopkins worked with Jared that day on more offensive line specific drills. Jared responded well to both Hopkins' and Hester's coaching and loved the idea of working with them more.

As much research as the Veldheers had put into finding the right agent and trainers, Hester had done his homework on Jared.

"I have worked with these agents for a long time and I am always pretty sure we aren't getting any 'head cases' sent our way. Still, I did some research, learned about how he ended up at Hillsdale, how he had done, and read good things about the type of kid he was," Kurt Hester explains.

The consensus at D1 was that they would be able to do a lot with Jared in his NFL Draft preparation if he were to choose Rick Smith as his agent. That consensus included Jared and before leaving Hopkins and Hester that day, Jared told them that he was done looking. D1 was the spot for him.

Jared waited to tell his family.

Later that evening, as Jim and Mary Veldheer were relaxing at the hotel and beginning to focus their attention on the meetings with Peter Schaffer in Miami, Jared told them they needed to talk.

Jared's mind was made up. He was confident that Rick Smith would do a good job representing him. He was even more convinced that D1 was the place where he needed to prepare for the Draft and he was certain Kurt Hester was exactly the kind of coach that would push him and get him ready for Indianapolis in February. He asked Jim if they could just go home. Jared was done. He was burnt out from Hillsdale's season and he was tired of the entire process. Sure, Miami and the Dolphins game sounded fun, but it made no sense to him to waste anymore of anyone's time when he was sure he had found what was best for him.

Jim called Smith and told him of Jared's decision. He then called to thank Schaffer for the offer and the opportunity but that Jared had already made his decision. There would be no trip to South Beach or suite tickets to the nationally televised Sunday Night NFL game, but there would be a lot of peace-of-mind at the Veldheer household heading into Christmas.

Chapter 18: Getting Technical

When Jared arrived at D1 in early January of 2010, reminders were everywhere that he was no longer in the Hillsdale College field house.

By all accounts, Jared never felt or acted like he didn't belong. Any nerves or worries he might have had were quickly put to rest.

"For me, I really had nothing to lose and when you get in the gym you're all the same size, you're just as strong as everybody," Jared said. "You're just as fast."

Trainer Kurt Hester echoed Jared in a Rivals.com article about the Hillsdale product training at the facility, "I think at first [the small-school players] might be a little uneasy being around guys from all these big programs and then after a week, they see they're just as strong, just as fast, just as athletic -- or more athletic."

Hester went on to tell Rivals.com that not only did

Jared belong in this group, there was something exceptional that he was seeing and he made some bold predictions about Veldheer.

"He'll blow the Combine up," Hester said. "He'll probably be the most impressive lineman there. He'll look like a (defensive back) compared to the tackles, he's so athletic. He'll just stand out because he moves like a skill player."

Brad Hopkins, the retired NFL veteran, would handle the lineman position work. He summed up why he thought the fitting-in process was no big deal for Jared, "Offensive linemen are all the same at heart. It doesn't matter where you played. We all think the same way. We're competitors and we have a job to do."

How would Jared's football technique match the guys from the big programs who had multiple coaches working with the offensive linemen?

"It was obvious that Jared had gotten some pretty good instruction at Hillsdale," Hopkins stated. "He was pretty sound technique-wise and you could tell he had worked really hard over the past four years. There was nothing he lacked that set him apart from the other guys."

While Jared was making it obvious that he belonged on the same field and in the same gym training next to Heisman Trophy winner Tim Tebow or Miami Hurricane Jimmy Graham, he also made it obvious that he was there to learn. Hopkins praised the attentiveness Jared showed in all aspects of his training while at D1, whether he was on the field working footwork or in the film room talking X's and O's.

"Any time I was showing him anything, I could tell that not only he was listening but that he was thinking about everything I was saying. And it's that attention to detail and doing everything...I call that 'playing through the whistle' that has allowed him to get where he is today."

His days at D1 would begin at 8:30 a.m. with most of the morning focus on speed. Some days would involve straight line, while others would focus on side-to-side and changing direction. The testing at the Combine would be assessing all of these abilities in events like the 40-yard dash and the various shuttle runs. In addition to just increasing pure speed, the staff at D1 focused hard on technique. At the Combine, fractions of seconds can mean the difference between millions of dollars when it comes to draft position. Those dollars are usually lost or gained in starts, stops, and changing direction. Learning how to master those techniques is just as critical as learning how to go fast. Peak performance in tests like the standing broad jump or the vertical jump also require learning a specific technique, such as coiling the right muscles and shifting weight at the right time during the initial explosion.

An additional part of performing well comes from increased flexibility. Wednesday mornings at D1 included extended sessions of yoga that were often followed by sports massage.

"It was killer," Jared intensely replied when this author even remotely suggested that the massage must have been comforting in rehabilitating the body. He wasn't meaning "killer" as in "awesome," "rad," "off the chain," or any of those other words the kids used to use.

"One day," he explained. "One of the therapists worked on my quadriceps for like an hour to an hour and a half. I had to play Words with Friends on my phone just to keep my mind off of the pain. It helped, but it hurt."

It was no spa indeed. Most details of day-to-day life for Jared and all of the other hopefuls were taken care of by D1 and the various agents. In addition to providing housing for the players, meals and nutrition were planned and prepared according to each athlete's individual needs.

Lunch was served daily at the facility. For Jared, it took extra large portions to maintain his weight at 315 pounds due to the tremendous amount of calories he was burning daily. Other players weren't as lucky and were still trying to shed pounds and trim up before the upcoming meat markets of all-star games and the Combine itself.

Jared said that there was always enough food to eat and everything provided was nutritionally balance, but on some evenings a quick walk for some ice cream over to Coldstone Creamery was the only thing that could satisfy Jared's hunger and need for calories.

Most afternoons featured excruciating strength workouts that alternated between upper body muscle groups one day and lower body muscle groups the next.

While most of the week was spent competing against oneself, Friday afternoon provided these elite athletes with the opportunity to compete against each other.

"Overall, it was an atmosphere of camaraderie among all of the guys but on Fridays when we would play Ultimate Frisbee," Jared explained. "It got really competitive."

As the Combine drew nearer, all of the training at D1 was taking Jared's body and agility to unexplored territory. Before Indianapolis however, he would experience the unexplored territory of another week-long audition, the College All-Star Game.

Chapter 19: Jared Versus the Nation

The start of February was a change of scenery for Jared as he traveled to El Paso for the Texas vs. The Nation game. Pro hopefuls were invited to the border city for a week's worth of practice and evaluation by scouts in a truer football setting than Combine drills. The game would feature a team of all Texas-born players against a team of players from all across the United States.

Just as Jared had seamlessly fit in with the group at D1, he fit right in among his Nation teammates despite being the guy with the least automatically recognizable helmet.

For Jared, going to El Paso was a lot like going to D1. Everyone had the same goal, same dream, and there were no more NCAA divisions. Getting back to playing football, Jared noticed his speed was one thing that would require an adjustment.

"Probably the biggest thing was the speed," he said. "But after getting used to that, it was a good week."

By most accounts, Jared had a great outing in El Paso. For much of the press that covers the Draft, this was their first look at Jared. Many articles began with a proclamation that this elusive small school athlete really did exist and that he was as athletic as advertised.

When game day arrived, it was pretty easy to spot Jared on the Nation team sidelines. Standing, what seemed at times a foot taller than some of the skill position players, Jared looked every bit as much of an NFL hopeful as his teammates from ACC and Big 10 schools did. For the Hillsdale fans watching on CBS College Sports across the country, it was a strange juxtaposition to see that royal blue helmet lined up next to ones from Tennessee and North Carolina.

Just as Jared had noticed the speed of the defenders on his Nation squad in practice, he would find the same to be true about the defensive players he would face from the Texas unit on Saturday. They were fast. Even though it was an exhibition, the speed of the game was even faster than the speed of practice.

As much as Jared had developed while at Hillsdale and perfected his technique with Brad Hopkins at D1, there were still moments in the game where one could see Jared still needed some polish. But just as he did early in the week, Jared adjusted. The draft commentators noticed he improved the more he was on the field.

An interesting battle began to develop late in the first half as Junior Gallette was placed outside to see what kind of pass rush he could get against Jared. Gallette was a half-foot shorter than Veldheer and at least fifty pounds lighter. Play after play, Jared showed he could handle the smaller speed rushers, bending at the knees to handle the more explosive players.

Just before the half, Gallette did something no other opponent had done against Veldheer since Forest Hills Northern High School; he got a sack. While Veldheer was escorting Gallette around the back of the pocket, Florida Atlantic quarterback Rusty Smith failed to step forward and Gallette took Smith to the turf.

Despite the sack, Jared's performance in the game and, overall, during his week in El Paso had been a success. Of all the 120 athletes at the Texas vs. the

Nation Game, it would be Jared Veldheer who would hear his name called first come draft day.

For the Veldheer family, it had been a memorable experience as well. Jared's parents were joined in El Paso by Jim's parents as well as Jared's Hillsdale teammate Aaron Waldie and girlfriend Morgan Podkul, a star Hillsdale athlete in her own right on the volleyball team.

For mom Mary, there was another special aspect of the trip, seeing Jared finally wear a jersey with his name on the back.

"Through all of the years of youth football, high school, and college Jared never wore a jersey with his name on it. Finally he did."

Chapter 20: NFL Combine 2010

After returning from El Paso, Jared spent the next two weeks fine-tuning at D1. Playing with a name on your jersey and on national TV would soon seem like a junior varsity game compared to performing at the Combine.

For whatever reason, football fans now set aside chunks of their February weekends to watch draft hopefuls run 40-yard dashes and take standing broad jumps.

The speed, strength, and agility tests are an important part of the players' time in Indianapolis, but just a sliver of what really happens. There are long days and nights being poked and prodded by doctors and constant meetings with coaches from all thirty-two teams. It can really take a toll on athletes physically and mentally.

"It is really an accomplishment when a guy is able to (test physically) really well at the Combine. You are on your feet going to team interviews, getting x-rays, getting prodded -- just hours before some of the tests like the 40 or the vertical leap," Jared shared about his experience.

Jared will be the first to tell you that he was somewhat disappointed by his 40 yard dash time of 5.09 after hoping to be in the 4.8-4.9 range. He was still fourth fastest amongst all of the linemen. Where Jared proved to be better than any other offensive line draft candidate assembled that week was in the short burst of speed, change of direction tests. The three-cone drill and the 20-yard shuttle both demanded these abilities and Jared turned in the quickest times in both drills.

After all of the testing, Jared would be the only lineman to place in the Top 10 in every skill evaluated. To go from the kid at football camps whose footwork was so bad that big schools had little interest in him to the man who had recorded the most complete physical performance of any lineman is a testament to all the work that Jared had put into the game of football and himself.

From all accounts, Jared was ramping up his draft stock in the team interviews as well. No one close to

Jared was surprised to hear he had nailed his Wonderlic intelligence test. He rumored as one of the all-time top grades ever earned at the Combine.

Jared made the most of his sit-down time with each team. After making the rounds with every club, Jared was called back by the Eagles and Saints and said that he enjoyed those longer sessions because he was able to watch some film with their coaching staffs and talk deep, deep X's and O's with people like coach Sean Peyton and his staff two weeks after the Saints had just won the Super Bowl.

If there was one area where Jared surprised the people who knew him best, it was the ease with which he handled the media. Jared has a great smile, but at times that is all he uses to express himself. He is a man of few words and even into his NFL career could come off as quite shy at times.

There was no shyness as he held court at a big round table in Indianapolis with the press. As reporters asked him about his experience at the Combine, how he had ended up at Hillsdale, and what he thought his potential in the NFL was, Jared used his big smile, looked every reporter in the eye, and gave crisp honest answers. It was as if he had been handling the media like this for years.

"I'm just taking it all in," Veldheer told reporters. "Coming here, a lot of guys say it stresses you out or wears on you. But it hasn't been that way at all for me. I'm absolutely loving this opportunity."

"It's definitely a surreal thing to think that I'm in this position. But then once you start thinking about it, I've worked very hard to be in the position I'm in right now."

Later, Jared's dad Jim would ask him if he had gone through special training at D1 on how to handle the media and where that ability had been developed. Jared just shrugged. No, there hadn't been any special training. That was just how Jared had always been raised to talk to people. You are polite and you give a straightforward answer. It seemed that simple.

With the grind of the Combine out of the way and another exceptional showing in this convoluted process under his belt, things were about to get really crazy for Jared and the Veldheers. Draft Day was six weeks away, but there was a lot to accomplish between leaving Indianapolis and learning his NFL fate.

Chapter 21: Grunts, Pro Day, and Nice Calves

It was back to reality for Jared once the NFL Combine ended. Jared's next month would be a whirlwind of activity, balanced between completing his degree, his Pro Day, touring NFL team facilities, and finally the Draft Day announcement of where he'd become a professional football player.

One of the biggest tasks he needed to accomplish in the coming weeks involved putting the student back in "student-athlete." Jared knew that the spring of 2010 was going to require large amounts of time away from Hillsdale, but he was determined to complete his biology degree by May. He had scheduled his course load so that all that was required of him was to finish his senior thesis.

Jared had come to Hillsdale to become a surgeon. Preparing for medical school was initially his big focus. If he had never developed into the prototypical NFL left tackle, chances are that he would still be able to distinguish himself as a doctor.

Jared's thesis however had nothing to with medicine, but one of his other passions in life—fishing. Hillsdale offers a three-week marine biology course every summer in the Florida Keys and Jared had focused on the digestive system of a species of snapper called the blue striped grunt.

Just because the NFL Combine was over, there was far more testing to come. In March, Hillsdale College would hold its first ever Pro Day. A Pro Day is when a number of teams send their scouts to watch a repeat of the Combine's on field testing on the player's home turf. This gives guys like Jared the chance to perform under much more familiar and favorable circumstances without the poking, prodding, and interviewing of the Combine. It also gives players not invited to the Combine a chance to perform in front of the scouts as well.

As Jared spent considerable amounts of time with fish guts in the lab, he spent the rest of it in the weight room with a special two-week workout regiment that D1 had prepared for him. It was more strength training, speed, and technique. His agent had told teams that Jared would be doing only position drills at Hillsdale and that they would let the Combine numbers speak for themselves.

As if that didn't take enough juggling, the St. Louis Rams, Kansas City Chiefs, and Philadelphia Eagles all sent their offensive line coaches to Hillsdale to meet with Jared one-on-one, see more lineman technique, and do more physical testing. Luckily for Jared he was able to keep the momentum going and continue his prescribed workouts.

Just as Jared had always been a team leader since his arrival in Hillsdale, he was sharing with the other pro hopefuls who'd perform at the Pro Day all of the little tips and techniques he had gleaned throughout the winter.

When that day finally arrived, one of the season's first glimpses of spring was in the air. The event was held outside in the sunshine and 55 perfect degrees. Representatives from nine teams had traveled to Hillsdale with the Ravens and Seahawks sending their line coaches. Jared went through all of the line drills as directed by the coaches, his footwork crisp, feeling at home on the turf where he had built himself into this key prospect. Teammates AJ Kegg, Mark Petro, and Drew Berube all excelled and each would earn rookie camp invites from the Browns, Jets, and Packers respectively.

With about three weeks before the Draft, Jared would complete an eight-day, 11,000-mile odyssey interviewing with teams and touring their facilities. The first leg would take him to meet with teams in Philadelphia, Denver, and San Francisco. Before jetting off to New York, Phoenix, and Oakland he would squeeze in a run down to Hillsdale to wrap up the biology thesis.

For Jared, the stop in Oakland was the most memorable for a number of reasons. First of all, the Raiders reserved a hotel that had been the nicest of any of the places Jared had stayed on his double cross-country trek. Second of all, he was booked in first class for the return flight...something anyone can appreciate but especially someone 6' 8", 315 pounds.

The best moment for Jared though was meeting legendary owner Al Davis. Just as Jared was about to leave, his host received a call that Mr. Davis wanted to meet Jared. The aging icon of the NFL came downstairs and was quick to show Jared his Super Bowl rings, stating he wanted another before it was his time to pass on. Jared politely said he hoped he had a chance to help make that happen. Then the unexpected happened as they shook hands and Jared stepped toward a cab to the airport.

"One more thing Eddie," Davis said. He called Jared "Eddie" because Jared's legal name is Edwin.

"Eddie, let me see your calves."

Jared paused but pulled up his pant leg to show the owner his calves.

"Nice."

Nice for Jared would be the next two weeks at home with his family. All of the big tests had been past. All that was left was to wait for the Draft to finally arrive.

Chapter 22: Draft Day

With Draft Day just a day away, it was time for the Veldheer family to make one last trip together before Jared would officially become a professional football player. Jared, sister Meghan, Mom, and Dad flew to New York City to enjoy some of the hoopla surrounding the early April circus that has evolved into the NFL Draft.

Jared had been invited to a special reception hosted by the NFL Players Association and would have a chance to mingle some of the biggest names ever to play football. After a little sightseeing in NYC, the Veldheers would return home to watch the Draft. Only the expected first rounders are invited to the actual selection ceremony held on the first night.

Jared's draft year would see the NFL stretch the Draft from its traditional two-day format to four days. Round one would be on primetime on Thursday night with rounds two and three on Friday night. The final four rounds would take place on Saturday. All would be televised on ESPN.

Jared spent Thursday afternoon as the guest on *The Huge Show* with Bill Simonson, a sports talk radio show broadcasted across Michigan. When asked what he was going to buy first with his expected signing bonus Simonson seemed somewhat taken aback by Jared's answer.

"Probably a hyperbaric chamber. I have been reading a lot about those lately and how they help with recovery from workouts and any injuries," Jared replied to the host who was probably expecting to hear something like a Cadillac Escalade or a nice house, not a machine that can speed healing by increasing oxygen levels to desired parts of the body.

Jared's dad Jim would later comment, "Only a biology major from Hillsdale would think of buying something like that with his first check."

On the first night of the Draft, four offensive tackles were selected, moving Jared closer to the top of the list of best players at that position still available.

When Friday arrived, it was more like Christmas Eve than some random day in early spring. Mary had the house looking festive with football decorations in preparation for a big celebration, complete with a local caterer Tommy Fitzgerald preparing a feast for fifty. Lots of family, high school and Hillsdale buddies would be arriving soon.

The basement would be the epicenter of the action that left the formal dining table as home to thirty-two NFL hats that Mary had recently purchased from the NFL store. There was one from each team, all in the identical style as the ones teams had handed the first rounders the night before at Radio City Music Hall. Jared would be ready to pop one on his head just as soon as he was picked, no matter what team it was. Thirty-one others would be returned.

Early in the evening, a local news crew stopped by to see how the NFL hopeful was holding up.

"It's crazy," Jared told Jack Doles from the Grand Rapids NBC affiliate. "You are sitting here with every pick and thinking 'if this team picks this guy, then this will happen when'...It's just kind of fun."

With all of the people who mattered most around him, Jared hunkered down for Rounds Two and

Three that Friday night. Of course he was nervous about when and if he would hear his name that night or if he would still be waiting on Saturday. His bigger worry was whether his cell phone would get enough reception on the lower level. He had made sure that his agent Rick Smith had given all of the teams his cell phone number as well as the Veldheer's home phone. The landline was the preferred number for an NFL coach to dial at selection time.

While the extended family, close friends from high school, and college teammates nervously talked about how the draft was panning out, Jared felt his phone buzz. Half surprised it was working downstairs, he stepped into a little exercise room for some quiet and to see who was calling from a number he didn't recognize.

"Hi Jared, this is coach Tom Cable. How would you like to be a Raider?"

Jared paused for a second. This was it. This was really happening.

"Absolutely," Jared replied. "That would be great."

While Jared spoke with his new head coach, murmurs of "Where's Jared?" began to echo through the watch party right about the same time that somebody close to the TV shouted, "Look."

ESPN had gone to a long commercial break and when they returned to live coverage, a handful of teams had made quick picks. There at the bottom of the screen, it read, "3rd Round, Pick #69, Oakland selection: Jared Veldheer, OT Hillsdale College."

A huge cheer filled the house at about the same time Jared and coach Cable finished their conversation. Jared stepped out of the little room and was mobbed by just about everyone present. The dream had become reality. All of the work, all of the planning had come to this. Jared Veldheer had just become one of the highest picked Division II players ever.

Back on ESPN, Chris Berman ran through the names of the recent picks and when he mentioned Jared from "little Hillsdale College where Chester Marcol once was a kicker" in his best Howard Cosell accent. He then asked resident draft guru Mel Kiper Jr., which of the picks he wanted to discuss. Kiper picked Jared. A graphic with a headshot of Jared along with all of the numbers from the Combine popped on the screen followed by highlights from Muddy Waters Stadium. As Kiper spoke, viewers watched Jared bullying GLIAC defensive linemen. Troy Weatherhead and Vinnie Panizzi even got themselves some time on ESPN as well.

Kiper gave his assessment of the Raiders' pick in his trademark, choppy bullet point cadence, "Six foot eight. 315 pounds. Team captain senior year. This guy was a veteran at the small college level, the Division II ranks, so obviously it's a big transition. The All Star game helped him I think. Showed he can step it up when challenged by better players. Thirty-three and a half vertical. Thirty-reps reps on the bench press. 5.05 forty. His computer numbers are outstanding."

"Now, short arms at 6' 8". Talking about a guy who checks in at 315 pounds. Can he get it done in the National Football League? That's the unknown. Can he overcome the short arms? You talk about keeping the defensive ends at bay. But he has great feet for a kid that size. He competes hard and I thought when you are talking about the third round area, that's a point in time because there's been a big drop off at the tackle after that first tier, earlier second tier group. That's the best on the board at that point and the Oakland Raiders desperately need help at tackle."

NFL Network was running its own Draft coverage simultaneously and analyst Mike Mayock gave his take saying, "I gave him a 3rd round grade at the Combine, but I still think he is a year to a year and a half to actually playing. He is a developmental prospect. Obviously, the question with all small school kids is 'Can he handle the competition?' I watched his tape from the All Star game he played in and I think he has an opportunity down the road to be a good football player."

When the pundits had moved onto a new set of prospects, Jared proudly placed his Raiders cap on his head while all of his Hillsdale buddies gathered around him and simultaneously broke into the Hillsdale College fight song just as they had done every time the Chargers had celebrated a victory.

As the party at the Veldheers made its way into the night, there was a definite sense of relief. There was no more waiting or guessing. That phase was complete—but a whole new phase was about to begin.

Chapter 23: Welcome to Raider Nation

The Oakland Raiders are synonymous with the founding of the American Football League in 1960 even though the upstart venture only added the franchise out of desperation when a Minneapolis-based owner jumped ship and joined the National Football League establishing the Vikings. The AFL gave Oakland the now empty slot and the rest is football history.

The Raiders stumbled in their first few seasons until new coach and general manager, Al Davis, was brought on to captain this pirate ship of a football team that had been taking on water the last few years. Despite recent struggles, since Davis's arrival in 1963 the Raiders have been one of the most successful franchises in the league with legendary figures like coach John Madden, Ken Stabler, Gene Upshaw, Otto Graham, Bo Jackson, and Marcus Allen. Thirteen former Raiders are enshrined in the NFL Hall of Fame.

Before his passing during the 2011 season, Al Davis took great pride in his renegade personality. He was counter-football-culture when the Bay Area was the epicenter of counter-culture in the 1960s. As the old Apple ad goes, he was, "not fond of rules and had no use for the status-quo." Neither do Raider fans, and they relish being just as different as the iconic owner. Long before seemingly every fan base started calling itself "Something-or-other Nation", Al Davis coined the term Raider Nation to describe the team's die hard fans in Oakland and across the world.

One week after the Draft, Jared was in Oakland and on the field with the Raiders as the team held its spring mini-camp. On day one, the team website featured Jared in his white number 68 jersey and trademark silver helmet with black stripe. Even more so than in Texas, Jared looked like he belonged. These players were all professionals now with no NCAA divisions to worry about, all together and all trying to make the same team.

Chapter 24: Hey Rookie

On Wednesday July 28th, 2010, the Oakland Raiders reported to the Napa, California Marriott to begin training camp. The franchise had been doing its preseason work in the heart of wine country for fifteen years and would be occupying the nearby middle school's two and a half fields for the next couple of weeks. For Jared, it would be a transformative month through camp and preseason.

As camp got underway, Jared paid close attention to the most basic technique fundamentals that had gotten him to Napa. He intently absorbed everything the Raider line coaches taught him, both technique and scheme-wise. He lived in offensive coordinator Hue Jackson's playbook and learned every player on the line's job. Since the beginning of this NFL journey, Jared had tuned out the doubters and was not going to let analysts on NFL Network or ESPN set his timetable. His goal was to help the Oakland Raiders win as soon as possible. He could best do that by finding a way to get on the field.

Early in camp, Jared's presence became known, and for the right reasons. He was tenacious on the field and a tireless worker off the field. His technique continued to improve and observers soon realized just how good he already was. When compared to the other Raiders on the offensive line, he was playing as well as anyone. The starting spot was clearly open to competition and there was a lot of speculation around who would be the 2010 starter.

In the heat of this position battle at tackle, Oakland made an announcement few saw coming, including Jared.

Instead of being groomed as the left tackle of the future, head coach Tom Cable announced that Jared would begin practicing as the team's center. If Jared would win the job, he would make NFL history as the largest man ever to play that position. At 6' 8", he would be two inches taller than the Ravens' Matt Kakula and former Raider center Don Mosebar both 6' 6".

Cable explained the decision, "He's cut differently.

He's a long-bodied, short-legged guy, so he's really closer to the ground than that 6' 8" look."

Jared would now be fighting it out with current center Samson Satele. It wasn't like Jared had never played the position before, but it had been a long time since he had snapped the ball to Mark Ehnis at Forest Hills Northern High School. Coaches continued to give Jared practice at tackle, keeping him sharp in case the experiment at center didn't play out as well as the team hoped.

When his first preseason game finally arrived, Jared and the rest of the Raiders were in Dallas and eager to hit someone in a different colored jersey. The last time Jared visited the state of Texas was to play in the All-Star game. The Texas vs. Nation in El Paso would seem like a sandlot compared to the audaciousness of Cowboys Stadium. Focused on the task at hand, Jared later admitted to Raiders.com that he was still a bit taken aback by his surroundings.

"There were a lot of butterflies. I was like, 'This is it. Cowboys Stadium.' I was standing out on the star during pre-game just taking it all in. After a few plays though you realize it's still just playing football."

Jared rotated with a number of players at both center and tackle. He got a huge surge while playing center and plowed a path for a beautiful quarterback sneak, so nice a handful of Raider bloggers called for him to be named the team's starter immediately.

Those writers wouldn't have to wait very long. A week later head coach Tom Cable would name Jared the team's starting center after a solid performance in the second preseason game at Chicago.

This big rookie from the little college had beaten both the competition and all of the predictions that he wouldn't be NFL ready for a couple of years.

Jared Veldheer was about to start in his first real NFL game. Jared's meteoric rise hit some turbulence that day in Nashville. The Raiders would face the Tennessee Titans week one of the season, just seventeen miles from the D1 facility where Jared had worked so hard preparing for the Combine.

Hillsdale College Football averaged 1,500 fans per

home game. Jared was about to find out what 70,000 hostile NFL fans sounded and felt like on his road trip to Tennessee for his first NFL regular season game.

The league's biggest center ever had two first half false start penalties and airmailed a snap over Jason Campbell's head. You can teach and simulate game-like situations, but you cannot fully replicate what 70,000 screaming fans do to your ability to hear the snap count out of a shotgun formation. The second half went much smoother for Jared but the Titans soundly beat the Raiders 38-13.

Every team starts the season full of optimism but this start could not have gone much worse for Oakland. It was time to "flush it," shake it off, and head home.

On Monday, coach Cable called Jared into his office and thanked him for the amount of work he had already contributed as a Raider. He had been asked to learn two positions, never complained, and was put directly in the lion's den at a spot he hadn't played since high school. The staff had re-evaluated their plans with Jared and decided that his upside as their left tackle of the future outweighed what he could deliver at center. Sampson Satele would start again at center and Jared would focus on left tackle.

Jared would share time at tackle for the next five weeks before winning the outright starting spot before the team's week seven trip to Denver.

His first start of his career at tackle would be one of his most memorable performances as a Raider. Watching Jared and his teammates on the offensive line obliterate the Bronco defense was like watching that Hillsdale homecoming game against Findlay. He completely manhandled whomever the Broncos sent his way. Darren McFadden would follow the rookie wearing number sixty-eight all afternoon. Once on an outside zone run and again on a screen pass where Jared drove Bronco Jarvis Moss all of the way into end zone, McFadden followed the cleared path. After that score, photographer Justin Edmonds would snap what would become a trademark pose of Jared celebrating the score with his arms raised in a big "V" against a backdrop of dejected Denver fans.

With the Raiders up 45-14 in the third quarter,

Center Sampson Satele would suffer a concussion. This forced Jared back to the middle to snap the ball. Go figure. He wouldn't even get to complete his first game as a starting tackle at that position. Now he was back in the position where he had struggled mightily six weeks earlier.

But like Jared had done so many times before on the football field, he flushed those memories of Tennessee and showed marked improvement at center as Oakland continued to roll. Shortly after Satele's injury, McFadden only needed one play to go fifty-seven yards right up the middle, off a Veldheer block. On that day, in the Mile High City, it didn't matter where Jared lined up; he was blowing open holes for Darren.

Jared would play every down that day and the Raiders left Denver with their biggest point total in franchise history, a 59-14 victory.

For Jared, he reveled in the team win but couldn't help but think about his luck.

"I had finally made it to being a starter at tackle," he

said. "We were just destroying them on the left side and they weren't changing their game plan a bit. Then Samson gets hurt and I move back to center. It was fun but I wanted to stay at tackle."

Other athletes might have sulked or made some public display claiming the team was wasting their talents by playing them out of their natural positions, but not Jared. That just wasn't who he was and it would not have helped the Raiders in any way.

Luckily Samson Satele's concussion was minor and he and Jared were able to return to their normal positions a week later and stay there for the rest of the season.

The Raiders would finish Jared's first season with eight wins and eight losses. It was a mediocre record but it ended a streak of seven straight losing seasons in Oakland. The Raider Nation knew they had something special in their new left tackle. After the season journalists would recognize Jared as a member of the AFC All-Rookie team.

Chapter 25: Leadership Can Be Lonely

Shortly after the 2010 season wrapped up, owner Al Davis fired Tom Cable as the Raiders' head coach. Offensive coordinator Hue Jackson took the reigns as the new head coach hoping to build upon the gradual success experienced in 2010.

Jared would be dealing with, for the first time in his career, adjusting to a new head coach and staff. Since Jackson was already the offensive coordinator, throughout the offseason Jared anticipated that much of the offense would remain the same.

On March 12, 2011, NFL players were officially "locked out" by owners. Collective bargaining could not produce a new agreement between teams and the players union, which led to no football for players and their respective teams. Athletes could not be in contact with team personnel and they could not use team facilities for training. There were no mini-camps or optional team activities. For many players in the league it was easy to slough off a little bit, but not for Jared.

Today, when Jared works with young athletes, one of the things he tells them is, "Leadership is lonely." In other words it's easy to gather a bunch of friends to go and goof-off. To be a leader means to do what your heart tells you is right and that isn't always attractive to the average person.

Jared knew how far he had come during that rookie season. In order to progress in the NFL, he was completely on his own. The last sixteen months had been a whirlwind working out for the Combine and then training with the Raiders. Not only had Jared gotten bigger, faster, and stronger, he had amassed an incredible amount of new knowledge in one of his life's passions, physical training. He had run it all through his scientific brain and wasn't about to keep it to himself.

The spring of 2011 was spent on campus at Hillsdale, not only training himself but putting pro hopefuls Andre Holmes and Troy Weatherhead through much of the same regiments Jared had done at D1 while preparing for the Combine. These two players had been as much a part of Hillsdale's resurgence as Jared had been. Sharing his knowledge of the process was both a joy for Jared and a sign of how much his teammates had meant to him. Both Weatherhead and Holmes would sign in April as undrafted free agents with an NFL team. Both would be cut in the preseason. Holmes, however, would eventually make his way to Oakland, reuniting with Jared prior to the 2013 season and become the Raiders' leading receiver in 2014.

The facilities at Hillsdale provided all of the training space and equipment he needed and Jared enjoyed spending time with his girlfriend Morgan as she finished her junior year. The familiar campus atmosphere was great, but as summer approached he began to think about creating his own facility close to home in Grand Rapids.

In May of 2011, Jared and his old quarterback Mark Ehnis launched a dream they had hatched one night at the card table. The two transformed an old auto glass shop into Power Strength Training Systems. For Jared, it was the perfect spot for him to not only focus and train but also to give him a chance to continue some of the strength coaching he had done that spring in Hillsdale. Today, area athletes from high school, college, and the pros come to train with Jared, and it's not just football players either. Volleyball teams, girls' soccer teams, and even elite hockey players have begun to realize how valuable the insight PSTS can provide them. For Jared, seeing lots of athletes using the facility is a joy.

Leadership wasn't completely lonely that summer as Jared would gain a training partner in Cameron Bradfield, Jacksonville offensive lineman at the time. The two had been rivals since high school. In 2011, they pushed each other through the responsibilities of preparing for a season with no team help.

Cam Bradfield states, "There are not enough great things I can say about Mark and Jared and how training at PSTS has helped my progress as an athlete. From day one I could sense a standard of quality and hard work that everyone brought to the table. Over time I could see myself getting stronger and pushing through new thresholds I had never met.

By the time I got to training camp, I knew I was physically stronger than I had ever been in my life and it showed."

When the labor dust settled and the 2011 NFL season started, it was apparent which athletes had lazily taken advantage of not being told what to do during the offseason and which ones, like Jared and Cam, had taken it upon themselves to continue improving themselves as athletes.

Despite being a second year player, Jared cemented his role as a leader for the Raiders through his work ethic. His steady demeanor and consistent increase in level of play helped the team deal with adjusting to a new coaching staff, the loss of Jason Campbell for the year at quarterback, and the sadness of the midseason death of long-time owner Al Davis. Rising above the adversity, the Raiders found themselves atop the AFC West at 7-4 on Thanksgiving weekend.

The highlight of the season, which seemed to garner the most national attention, was Jared's play against the Vikings' perennial All-Pro defensive end Jared

Allen. Coming into the game, Allen had recorded at least one sack in his previous eleven games. Veldheer would put a stop to that and his efforts would not go unnoticed.

Quarterback Carson Palmer was quick to share his thoughts on his young tackle's accomplishment, "I don't think it hit him. Not many guys play that well against that guy, and he didn't have any help either. We came in and put him one-on-one, didn't put a tight end on his side to help. The coaches asked before the game if he was up to the challenge, and he said yeah. He was, obviously."

Veldheer was quick to share any accolades with teammates, "Every person on the O-line plays a role in that. Every person on the offense plays a role in that, because we weren't living in 3rd-and-long much. That helps. And being able to operate the no-huddle like Carson does helps. To sit here and say what I did doesn't do all of those things justice."

Adding to the momentous occasion was the fact that fifty of the Veldheer's relatives, most who live in South Dakota, had made the game into a family reunion and were able to watch their favorite Raider have a spectacular day.

Despite the hot start, the team would lose four of its last five games, finishing the season a mediocre eight and eight for the second straight year.

Somewhere among the rough patches of the final weeks came a very special moment for the Veldheers. The Raiders had just lost a home game to the Detroit Lions. That unhappiness faded quickly as later that night Jared asked Morgan to marry him. He had planned on proposing down on the field at the Coliseum, but after the team blew a thirteen point lead in the final minutes of the game, he figured it was better to pop the question later that night at Ruth's Chris restaurant in San Francisco.

For management, the end of season collapse was unacceptable. Hue Jackson and his staff were fired eleven days after the season.

Chapter 26: Starting All Over Again

Summers go quickly for NFL players. As July wound down, it was back to the West Coast for Jared. He had put a lot of work into the 2012 offseason while training with the crew at Power Strength. He'd also done a little "giving back" to the community by hosting free youth football camps on both sides of the state of Michigan.

After helping get the Raiders one game away from the playoffs two seasons in a row, he was determined to do all he could to help get his team over the hump.

The intensity with which Jared was attacking the upcoming season was evident in one of his first interviews after arriving in Napa for training camp. He sat down with San Jose reporter Monte Poole and showed that behind that big smile and gentle demeanor rests a warrior.

"You take pride in being able to sustain a block, to

finish it, to get people on the ground," he says, grin expanding. "As an offensive lineman, it's one of the best feelings there is. That's when it's the most fun. Whether it's driving someone down on a zone (run) play or if it's dropping back and finishing someone in pass protection, it's always one of the best feelings in the game. That, and when you get a good shot on someone when you're helping out."

There would be a ton of adjustments to handle that training camp and it was almost like being a rookie again. Dennis Allen, the new head coach, was Jared's third head coach in three years. Jared had to adapt to the new offensive approach Allen brought to the team, which looked nothing like the scheme they had previous seasons.

At least running back Darren McFadden seemed as fast as ever when camp began.

"He really makes us all look good," Jared would comment one day after an early camp practice.

Unfortunately, Darren McFadden would be lost halfway through the year and the Raiders would limp to a four and twelve record. Both the offense and defense would rank near the bottom of the NFL.

After Tom Cable and Hue Jackson had both lost their jobs for producing eight and eight seasons, speculation ran rampant the first Monday after the 2012 season ended about the fate of Dennis Allen who had only won four.

On New Year's Eve, 2012 the Raiders announced that both Allen and new general manager Reggie McKenzie would remain, but that several other coaches including Jared's line coach Frank Pollack had been fired.

Oakland made it clear that in order to turn around the losing and mediocrity, a number of Raiders had played their last ball games in silver and black. McKenzie would be cleaning house in the offseason. By the time the 2013 season rolled around, very few of the guys who had been on the team when Jared arrived would still be on the roster.

Hopefully for Jared, the Raiders, and the rest of the fanbase, the house cleaning would pay off in

better-disciplined play and most importantly more
wins.

Chapter 27: The Hulk Goes Viral

2012 was a tough one to endure for a team that seemed so close to getting over the hump. Despite only winning four games, Jared still had a season of tremendous growth. He not only stood out as the team's best lineman, he stood out as one of the top players on the team.

Pro Football Focus stated in its post-season rankings of all thirty-two offensive lines, "There is but one stud on this line, and his name is Jared Veldheer. Emerging as one of the better left tackles in the league, he's not quite lockdown yet, but he's pretty close."

Jared would split time between California and Michigan that spring of 2013. When he wasn't in Oakland doing team activities, he was back in Grand Rapids training at Power Strength with Mark, or helping Morgan get everything in order for their June wedding.

Toward the end of March, one post-workout tweet from Mark Ehnis would change everything. Jared Veldheer would become a viral Internet sensation when a picture from a grueling lifting sessions began bouncing around the World Wide Web.

The sheer mass of Jared's arms and chest in that picture as well as the way he dwarfed the three other large men in it seemed nearly super-human. The picture traveled the Internet so fast that it soon was featured on the front of several major sports sites like Yahoo Sports, CBS Sports, and USA today. After the first wave seemed to settle a bit, a second viral picture began making its way across the Internet. Someone had taken the picture into a photo editor and had colored Jared green and made his shorts purple to resemble "The Incredible Hulk."

On the Raiders' website, Jared would elaborate more on the picture and give a lot of credit to the focus he had put on nutrition that spring, "I've always stayed disciplined in my workouts, but I really started watching my nutrition and really making sure I was eating well in relation to before the workout, after the workout, all that stuff. I think I've seen some good strength gains by doing that. I've always heard it's really important, and I really started being disciplined in doing that."

The picture had found so much traction that when the post-draft mini camp convened three weeks later, Jared would field one question after the next about what he had done to achieve those results and if he felt bulking up too much would effect his play.

"Contrary probably to what a lot of people think, I've been able to keep working on flexibility and my range of motion," said Veldheer. "I've been working on offensive linemen stuff as well. We try to incorporate line skill work into the end or beginning of the workouts. That might be working on explosive pass sets with resistance bands or after an upper body day, working on your punch against the bag for time – really trying to get as many punches in as you can, good punches, working on your hands that way, all the kinds of stuff that translates directly to what I do as an offensive lineman. It's not all just straight weight lifting and it's all stuff that transfers over to the field."

Jared and Morgan were married in late June. Jared's brother Aaron would serve as the best man and in his toast told the newlyweds, "Stay in the game. Just like in football, there will be good times and not so good times. Stick with it. Learn as you go and if you stay in the game, you two will have a great life together."

Aaron had become more than Jared's brother or his best man. Shortly after the 2012 season, Jared parted ways with Rick Smith and had hired Aaron as his agent. With 2013 being Jared's final year of his rookie contract, Aaron would begin the negotiation process with the Raiders shortly after the wedding. Oakland would be the only team allowed to talk new contract with Jared until March of 2014. If no new deal was in place by then, Jared would become an unrestricted free agent and allowed to join any of the other thirty-one teams. His performance during the upcoming season would largely determine his demand on the free-agent market and future salaries.

Just as Jared had been eager to end the college recruiting roller coaster quickly, he was just as eager to end the contract uncertainty. He was optimistic that something could be sewn up prior to the season. He was hopeful after members of Raiders management stated they wanted to make Jared the cornerstone of their rebuilding process, which made re-upping seemed like it should be an easy process.

"Jared is really comfortable in Oakland," his dad Jim shared. "He likes the people at the facility, the other linemen, and where he lives in Dublin, California."

Mark Davis, the owner of the Raiders, had a special bond with the Veldheer family. As nice as a comfort level can be, the ultimate motivation for Jared was to do all he could to help turn around the franchise that had brought him to the National Football League. He knew that selecting a Division II player had been a gamble for Al Davis and Tom Cable and since day one. Jared was determined to prove he had been a wise choice for the organization.

Tuning out all of the noise had always been a special trait that propelled Jared toward success. After three head coaching changes, four different offensive line coaches in four years, and coming off a 4-12 record, most players would have found a shrine and lit a candle to St. Jude the patron of lost causes. Jared didn't see it that way. He was continually optimistic. He envisioned something similar to the turn-around he helped lead in college.

Solely focused on making that happen, Jared would let Aaron and the team executives worry about contracts. There was another season of football to play.

Chapter 28: Bad News from Napa

The 2013 Oakland Raiders' season began with the team's arrival in late July to its training camp in Napa, California. Similar to every other year of Jared's tenure in Oakland, there were a lot of new faces in camp.

The Raiders had traded quarterback Carson Palmer to the Cardinals for draft picks and had given Seattle a 2013 fifth-round pick for Matt Flynn to replace him.

Keeping everyone healthy in training camp is always a priority, especially to a franchise that had seen several of its recent seasons compromised due to losing key players to injuries.

With Jared however, the Raiders coaches never had reason to be concerned about injuries. He had missed only one practice in five years at Hillsdale and had played in all forty-eight games as a Raider, starting the last forty-two straight. When Jared developed soreness in his left elbow and had to miss practice to get an MRI during the second week of training camp, the coaching staff took immediate notice as did the media and Raider fans everywhere.

Raider Nation breathed a sigh of relief when team physician Dr. Warren King reported the MRI showed no damage in the triceps area. For the next ten days Jared wore a heavy elbow brace, never missed a practice, and played in the team's preseason opener against the Cowboys.

After experiencing no improvement, Jared left camp and went into the Bay Area for a second MRI. In a higher quality image, Doctor King located a partial tear in the tendon that connected Jared's triceps muscle to his elbow. Within two days, Dr. Neal *ElAttrache* performed surgery on the torn tendon in Los Angeles. Dr. ElAttrache is the same doctor who had recently repaired Dodgers' pitcher Zack Greinke's shoulder and Laker Kobe Bryant's Achilles tendon.

Following surgery, Jared began a three-month rehabilitation process. Oakland had placed their left tackle on the NFL's "injured reserve, designated for return" list. A typical injured reserve designation makes a hurt player ineligible for the remainder of the season. Jared's exception would allow the Raiders to free up a roster spot until he was medically cleared to resume football activities. If all went well, Week Thirteen's Thanksgiving Day game in Dallas would be Jared's 2013 regular season debut.

The Raiders needed all of the help they could get. When they finally welcomed Number Sixty-Eight back to the lineup the team was struggling at 4-8. McFadden was injured again. Flynn had lost the starting job in training camp to Terrelle Pryor. Flynn was cut four games into the season to make room for Jared's old Hillsdale teammate Andre Holmes, and Matt McGloin had recently replaced Terrelle Pryor.

Having Jared back in the lineup for Oakland added an extra dose of holiday cheer for Raider fans. More importantly, it gave quarterback Matt McGloin more confidence.

"It's great to see Jared back," McGloin told ESPN. "He's such a great part of that line and he has been since he's been here."

For Hillsdale College fans, seeing Veldheer and Holmes in the starting lineup was historical. Never before had two players from that little college ever played in the same game as professionals, let alone on the same team.

Jared knew he would be rusty, but also knew he was better rested than the competition heading into the final stretch of the season. What he might have lacked in polished technique he made up for in stamina, playing every offensive snap and keeping Pro Bowl end DeMarcus Ware completely in check.

Meanwhile, the other guy from Hillsdale was an absolute star that day. Despite the Raiders losing 31-24, Andre Holmes had his biggest day as a pro. Holmes caught seven passes for 136 yards. In the process, announcers Jim Nantz and Phil Simms repeatedly discussed the Hillsdale College football program that Andre and Jared led to their first ever Division II playoff appearance. Coincidentally, it was fellow GLIAC star Brandon Carr from archrival Grand Valley State University who was consistently burned by Holmes. Carr would have the last laugh; however, as he intercepted McGloin to seal the Dallas win.

Unfortunately, the spark of Jared's return to the lineup did not ignite a Raiders' hot streak. Oakland lost its remaining games to finish 4-12 for the second straight year.

Chapter 29: The Business of Sports

Jared Veldheer has never been one to leave any task undone. Whether or not he would have the opportunity to help bring the Raiders more wins would depend on a number of factors. The ball was now in the team's court.

Oakland could re-sign Jared to a new deal at any time between December 30 and March 10. The Raiders also had the option of placing a one-year franchise tag on Jared during a two-week window in late February and early March. The franchise tag allows teams to restrict a player from becoming a free agent, but the team has to pay that player the average of the top five salaries being paid to players at his position. Experts estimated that would run the Raiders roughly $12,600,000 in salary for one year of Jared's services. The final option for Oakland was to allow Jared to become a free agent in March and see what other teams might offer on the open market.

Oakland chose this final option. Jared became an unrestricted free agent, which came to surprise for teams around the league.

"We were shocked, shocked," Arizona offensive coordinator Harold Goodwin would tell the "Arizona Republic."

The team didn't think there would be any way Oakland would let Jared possibly reach the open market as a free agent.

It also didn't take long for former Raider and now Cardinal quarterback Carson Palmer to call general manager Steve Keim and head coach Bruce Arians, urging them to pursue signing Jared to be his new left tackle.

As time ticked off toward Saturday, the day when other teams could begin to contact Jared, the Cardinal brain trust began to do its homework. Keim and Arians watched a lot of film on Jared but already knew the kind of player he was from facing Oakland at various times over the course of the last few years. Although Keim didn't become general manager until

January of 2013, he had been in the organization for a decade and a half. Arizona was one of the stops on the whirlwind pre-draft tour Jared had taken and Keim had done a lot of evaluating of the prospect out of Hillsdale. Cardinals cornerbacks coach Kevin Ross was also called into discussion. He was the defensive backs coach in Oakland the year the Raiders drafted Jared.

After establishing what the team thought was a pretty good profile of Jared as a potential Cardinal, Keim went back to Carson Palmer just to confirm the findings.

Palmer would later tell the press, "Steve had asked me a handful of questions that he'd already known the answers to, really. He had done plenty of research and turned over every stone. He asked me questions where he kind of stated the answer and I just kind of said, 'Yeah, that's correct. That's correct. That's correct.' There is nothing you can say negative about it. It's easy to find those things in free agency because everyone is looking for a flaw, but what you see is what you get with Jared. Old school."

While Jared would not be able to sign a contract with anyone but Oakland until Monday, March 11, Aaron's phone rang on Saturday the 9th. As soon as league rules allowed, Steve Keim was making his sales pitch to the Veldheers that Jared should spend the next several years as a member of the Arizona Cardinals.

At 1:00 p.m. Arizona time on Monday, March 11, the Cardinals announced they had come to terms with their new left tackle Jared Veldheer. Within minutes of the announcement Cardinals president Michael Bidwill was cleared for takeoff in his private jet. He was headed to Grand Rapids, Michigan to pick up Jared, Morgan and Aaron Veldheer.

A celebration much smaller than the one the they'd hosted on Draft Day got underway at Jared's parents' house, which had served as the hub of negotiations. Jared, his wife Morgan, Aaron, and his wife Jodi raised their glasses in a toast to end of negotiations and a future in Arizona. In a couple of hours Jodi would bid the other three safe travels as they boarded the jet and sped off for the Sonoran Desert.

The three Veldheers relaxed, but also tried to process this crazy journey and the fact that Jared would soon sign a contract worth $35,000,000. Once the plane got up to cruising altitude and Bidwill's co-pilot took over, the owner ventured back to visit with his passengers and new left tackle.

Once on the ground in the Phoenix area, Keim and Arians took Jared out for a big steak. Keim would quip the next day that Jared was the first free agent the team had signed who could eat more than him.

Chapter 30: What it is all About

After completing his physical and touring the team's Tempe facility, Jared Veldheer appeared at a large table with Morgan by his side. Together, they had picked out a new red tie just for the occasion. After signing the new contract, the Cardinals officially introduced Jared Veldheer as their team's new left tackle.

After introductions were complete, Jared offered the following statement, one that sums up who he is what in his life matters most.

"OK, first I'd just like to start off with a couple of thank-you's. I just want to thank God, first and foremost, for all the blessings He's given me and allowing me this opportunity to come to Arizona and be with this great organization.

Secondly, I'd like to thank the Bidwill family, Steve Keim and Coach Arians for believing that I'm a guy that can really help this team and be one of those pieces to get us to the playoffs and to a championship.

Then, also I'd like to thank my wife, Morgan, who is standing there in the back, for her love and support along this whole process, all the encouragement that she's given me and all the sacrifices she's had to make along the way the past few years; never easy and she does a great job putting up with me, so I'd like to thank her.

I also thank my mom and dad for all their support along the way. Their constant love and encouragement really meant a lot to me, always encouraging; when I was down would lift me up. I really appreciate them and everything they've done.

I'd like to thank my sister Meghan for having to share the spotlight with me through my NFL career. I know it's not hard because she's a college volleyball player. It's tough sometimes sharing the sibling spotlight like that, but she does a great job, and she's very positive. She'll be successful in whatever she chooses to do.

And, I'd like to thank my brother, Aaron, who's also in the back of the room, for his hard work and helping me along this process, and ultimately guiding me where I needed to go."

Afterward

In 2014, Jared Veldheer quickly became recognized as a key leader on the Cardinals offense. His locking down the left tackle position afforded the team new options in both the passing and power running game.

Jared's reunion with his former quarterback Carson Palmer would help lead to one of the most exciting regular seasons in Arizona Cardinals history. The 11-5 record was the franchise's highest win total since 1975 and would take them somewhere Jared had never been, the NFL Playoffs.

Despite the impressive record, the Cardinals faced their share of adversity. It looked like the Palmer-Veldheer reunion might only last one game. Palmer injured his shoulder in a Week One win over San Diego. The team never missed a beat though as backup Drew Stanton would win two of the next three before Palmer returned to win five straight and move Arizona's record to 8-1. Week Nine would prove costly though. Despite a win over St. Louis,

Palmer would injure his left knee and be lost for the year. Stanton took over and beat the Detroit Lions to move the team to 9-1 and atop the NFC.

From there momentum waned and the Cardinals would lose two of their next three before Stanton too would be lost for the season due to a knee injury. Too many injuries doomed the team as they would limp out of the postseason with a loss to the Carolina Panthers in the first round of the playoffs.

Through it all, Jared maintained the exact same focus he had since high school.

"Control what you can control," he tells kids when asked what one of the most important things he does as a player. Jared couldn't get caught up in worrying about who would play quarterback. All he could do was make sure he and the rest of the offensive line were doing their jobs and giving whoever was back there all of the time they needed to throw the ball.

Jared would eventually be recognized as the cornerstone who held it all together for the Cardinals in 2014. Shortly after the season, Arizona sports writers voted him as the recipient of the Lloyd Herberg Most Valuable Player Award. According to reporter Mike Jureki, the award is named for Lloyd Herberg, who covered the Cardinals for The Arizona Republic.

The Cardinals seemed to agree. As the team broke training camp for the 2015 season, Jared was named an offensive captain along with Carson Palmer. He and the rest of the leaders in the organization would go on to take Arizona all of the way to the NFC Championship Game before falling to Carolina in what was truly a spectacular season.

Since his first season in Arizona, Jared has begun to settle into the community and desert lifestyle. He is a frequent guest on sports radio shows where he will talk about anything from the Cardinals to how his Hillsdale College degree in science helps him control all of the variables in his home beer brewing process. You might find Jared throwing out the first pitch at an Arizona Diamondbacks game or waving the checkered flag at a NASCAR race.

Jared also gives back to the community by raising money for the Pat Tillman Foundation, saluting our United States men and women in uniform, and helping spread his love for football at youth camps around the state.

In May of 2015, Jared and Morgan Veldheer welcomed their first child into the world, a little girl named Eva Victoria Veldheer. If you follow his social media accounts it is quite apparent Jared loves being a dad.

Wherever life will take Jared after football is yet to be determined. You can bet that the key principles that have made him a successful football player and young man will be leading the way.

•Stay in the Game•

Five of life's most important principles that made Jared a great football player and can make anyone great at whatever they choose to do.

1. God has a plan for your life.
2. Choose your friends wisely.
3. Listen to your coaches and those you trust. Tune out all the other noise.
4. Set goals. Track your goals. Achieve your goals.
5. Learn from your mistakes but don't dwell.

Jared leads members of the Cardinals and Panthers in prayer after the 2016 NFC Championship Game. (Photo Kelsey Riggs - WCNC TV Charlotte)

All proceeds from *Stay in the Game* go to support not-for-profit organizations and programs committed to helping kids.

Jared Veldheer may be contacted through his marketing representative Brian Bradtke at B2 Enterprises
www.b2-enterprises.com
info@b2-enterprises.com

Andy Losik is a 1994 Hillsdale College graduate. Shortly after his playing days, he built *chargerblue.com* on a very primitive mid 1990's Internet in order to share his passion for the program and College. The site has gone on to become the longest continuously run Division II football site on the web. It was through "Chargerblue" that Andy became friends with the Veldheer family early in Jared's career at Hillsdale. First and foremost Andy Losik is dad and husband who also teaches technology classes in Hamilton, Michigan..

Jim Veldheer has been a Financial Advisor at Merrill Lynch for 25 years.

Mary Veldheer has her Masters in Social Work and is a community volunteer.

Check out our Facebook page for more pictures and to share your comments on *Stay in the Game.*
Just search "Jared Veldheer Stay in the Game".